Psychology of the Mexican

CULTURE AND PERSONALITY

The Texas Pan American Series

Psychology of the Mexican

CULTURE AND PERSONALITY

by R. Díaz-Guerrero

UNIVERSITY OF TEXAS PRESS, AUSTIN

The Texas Pan American Series is published with the assistance of a revolving publication fund established by the Pan American Sulphur Company.

Previously published as *Estudios de psicología del mexicano*
© 1967, Editorial Trillas, S.A.

Library of Congress Cataloging in Publication Data

Díaz Guerrero, Rogelio.
  Psychology of the Mexican: culture and personality.

  (The Texas pan American series)
  Translation of Estudios de psicología del mexicano.
  Bibliography: p.
  Includes index.
  1. National characteristics, Mexican. I. Title.
[DNLM: 1. Ethnic groups—Mexico—Essays. 2. Ethno-
psychology—Mexico—Essays. BF755.M6 D542p]
BF755.M4D513   155.8′9′72   74–23309
ISBN 978-0-292-76430-9

CONTENTS

Introduction xi
1. Neurosis and the Mexican Family Structure . . . 3
2. Mexican Assumptions about Interpersonal Relations . 17
3. Motivations of the Mexican Worker 21
4. The Mental, Personal, and Social Health of the
    Mexican of Mexico City 48
        Appendix 1. A Definition of Mental Health, p. 69
        Appendix 2. The Tools of the Research, p. 74
5. Two Core-Culture Patterns and the Diffusion of
    Values across Their Border 78
6. Respect and Status in Two Cultures 89
7. Sociocultural Premises, Attitudes, and Cross-Cultural
    Research 112
8. The Passive-Active Transcultural Dichotomy . . . 127
9. Problems and Preliminary Results of Sociopsychological
    Research in Mexico 134
10. Exploring Dimensions in Socioeconomic
    Development 145
Bibliography 157
Index 165

TABLES

1-1. Degree of Mental Health 11
1-2. Sociocultural Premises (Values) 13
1-3. Percentage of Affirmative Responses of Mexicans and
      Puerto Ricans to Questions Related to
      Sociocultural Premises 16
4-1. Tentative Questions in Categories 1 and 2 (Tolerance
      and Objectification of the Ego) 58
4-2. Tentative Questions in Category 3 (Ability to See Proj-
      ects of Delayed Realization, "Reality Principle") . 58
4-3. Tentative Questions in Category 4 (Incapacitating or
      Distressing Mental Symptoms) 59
4-4. Tentative Questions in Category 5 (Inhibition of
      Behavior Provoked by Sociocultural Norms) . . 59
4-5. Tentative Questions in Category 6
      (Ignorance and Animism) 60
4-6. Adult Population of Mexico City in July, 1948,
      Classified by Occupation 61
4-7. Percentage of Cooperation by Areas in Order of
      Diminishing Percentage 61
4-8. Answers to Questions in Categories 1 and 2
      (Tolerance, Objectification of the Ego) . . 62
4-9. Answers to Questions in Categories 1 and 2
      According to Sex 62
4-10. Answers to Questions in Category 3 (Ability to See Proj-
      ects of Delayed Realization, "Reality Principle") . 63

4-11. Answers to Questions in Category 3 According to Sex . 64

4-12. Answers to Questions in Category 4 (Incapacitating or
   Distressing Mental Symptoms) 65

4-13. Answers to Questions in Category 4 According to Sex . 65

4-14. Answers to Questions in Category 5 (Inhibition of
   Behavior Provoked by Sociocultural Norms) . . 66

4-15. Answers to Questions in Category 5 According to Sex . 67

4-16. Answers to Questions in Category 6
   (Ignorance and Animism) 67

4-17. Answers to Questions in Category 6 According to Sex . 68

5-1. Subject-Sample Sizes 80

5-2. Analysis of Variance for Item 1: An Illustration . . 82

5-3. Percentages 83

5-4. Respect: The "Core-Culture" Pattern in Mexico
   and in Texas 84

5-5. Diffusion of Values 86

6-1. Cosmos of Respect in Mexican Society
   (Male Preparatory Students) 96

6-2. Cosmos of Respect in American Society
   (Male Undergraduate Students) 97

6-3. Cosmos of Respect in Mexican Society
   (Female Preparatory Students) 98

6-4. Cosmos of Respect in American Society
   (Female Undergraduate Students) 99

6-5. Transcultural Comparison: Male Preparatory Students
   in Mexico and Male Undergraduates in
   the United States 100

6-6. Transcultural Comparison: Female Preparatory
   Students in Mexico and Female Undergraduates
   in the United States 106

7-1. Percentages of Agreement with Statements . . 115

9-1. Sociocultural Premises about the Mother and
   the Feminine Role 136

9-2. Sociocultural Premises about the Father and
   the Masculine Role 137

9-3. Sociocultural Premises about Both Parents
       and the Family   137
9-4. Motivations for Working: Paired Comparison Study   .   143
10-1. Affective Meaning of Work   150
10-2. Motivations for Working: Paired Comparison Study   .   151
10-3. Sociocultural Premises   153

FIGURE

3-1. Hypothetical Profile of the Motivation of the
       Mexican Worker   47

INTRODUCTION

There is a world of difference between Carlos Castaneda's *Teachings of Don Juan* and Oscar Lewis's studies of the anthropology of poverty. Erich Fromm and Michael Maccoby reveal yet another world in their study, *Social Character in a Mexican Village*.

In the introduction to the first Spanish edition of this book, I wrote: "As time passes, my conviction increases that the just or unjust, complete or incomplete evaluation that will be made of the Mexican people will depend primarily upon the nature of the conceptual approach utilized by the investigator." I pointed out that the description of the Mexican can vary significantly according to the approach used: psychological, phenomenological, and anthropological approaches can yield very different results. I also conceded the dangers of stereotyping the people of a country as luxuriantly diverse in its population as is Mexico. Finally, I indicated that the studies that appeared in that edition (the first four in the present volume) were merely methodological probes, each utilizing a distinct procedural method.

Still, although the methods and objectives of the four studies were distinct, the reader will be struck by the degree to which these studies coincide in portraying something that could certainly be called "Mexican," as opposed to something else that could be called "Anglo-American."

The story is quite different with the additional studies included in the second and third Spanish editions (Essays 5–10 of this volume). The optimal methodology is becoming clear. We are dealing with the effects of culture upon personality. The conceptual approach, therefore, is historico-psycho-bio-sociocultural; that is, we are dealing with historical, psychological, biological, social, economic, and anthropological variables. We must assume, first, that Mexicans have something in common; second, we must develop ways to measure this shared area; and, third, we must also develop ways to measure variations from the general pattern produced by psycho-biological variables, such as age; by social-status variables, such as socioeconomic levels; and by historico-bio-sociocultural variables, such as sex and social change.

The methodology, with one difference, is that of the behavioral sciences. The data have been gathered and analyzed in accordance with the strict standards of scientists well known for their highly ethical attitude toward these matters; I would like to acknowledge particularly the help of Drs. Wayne H. Holtzman, Robert F. Peck, Charles E. Osgood, and Carl F. Hereford. As for the interpretation of the data, I follow the usual procedures of hypothesis testing and limited inferences from the proven hypothesis. At this point, however, I permit myself, on the basis of large amounts of data, to formulate certain broad conceptual schemes. These conceptual schemes have immediate application to the understanding of human behavior in real life situations and, particularly, to what might be called the wisdom of living. I am interested in discovering the ways in which the data are particularly relevant in the life of the individual as he relates to the significant people in his environment: members of his family, friends, sweethearts, community, society, nation, humanity.

I might mention, as a kind of validation, that my lectures before the people of the culture or cultures for which I interpret the data are usually enthusiastically received. People speak of their sense of having been clearly described, both as individuals and as groups. They often add that they have a better understanding of the workings of their own culture and that they see their own behavior more objectively and as part of a rational system.

Such statements should not mislead the reader into believing that we are dealing with something simple and easily evident. Actually, in order to advance in this rather complex field it has been necessary to take several steps: first, the assumption of an ad hoc theory of culture; then, the development of what psychologists call theoretical operational constructs to use in the study of the effects of culture upon personality; and, finally, the carrying out of a substantial number of comparisons, involving from one to twenty-three different nations. As we proceed, we realize that there are a number of levels on which we can understand the functioning of cultures and their effects upon the individuals and groups exposed to them through history.

Let me dramatize, using unpublished data, the interplay of a few factors that seem to characterize and explain the behavior of individuals and groups in Anglo, Mexican-American, and Mexican societies. I believe that, if you read the rest of this book with this conceptual pattern in mind, you will better understand each of the studies between its covers.

It is said that in the thirty-third year of our Lord a Mexican visited Jerusalem. On the day he arrived, there was a great commotion in the streets. Hoards of people were moving in one direction. Guided as always by the wisdom of his people, the Mexican thought, "Where are you going, Vicente? Where all the people are going!" He joined the crowds and with them arrived before a disturbing spectacle. There, on a hill, a man was hanging on a cross. The Mexican said, "Look what they are doing to the Lord!" He rushed toward Jesus Christ and pulled out the nail that held one of his hands. He immediately went to the other side and pulled out the other nail. Jesus Christ, held by the nails in his feet, clawed the air in desperation and fell face forward with a crash.

The moral is that love is fine, but it must be efficacious love. On the other hand, there is the statement of a wise old Mexican, who said during the government of one of the Mexican presidents: "Dios nos libre de los pendejos con iniciativa." The Spanish expression has more impact than its English equivalent, but might be translated as "There is nothing so dangerous as a fool in power." Power, too, as Americans are becoming more and more aware, may be efficacious or inefficacious.

Historically these two rather dramatic dimensions of human behavior, love and power, have affected people independently of each other. Jesus Christ died on a cross and brought about a profound revolution of love. Marx and Engels initiated a profound revolution of power. Both revolutions seem to have overlooked what every human being in the street knows, that both the need for love and the search for power exist, and that human relations *as they are* cannot be produced or explained by either factor alone. We must try to deal with both of them and with their interactions if we are to make any sense of human behavior.

Two historical patterns—that of the United States of Mesonorthamerica[1] and that of Mexico—and the cultures that they gave rise to clearly illustrate the need for more comprehensive schemes, if we are to understand cultural differences and cultural patterns.

An interesting fact emerges: much of what we have been able to determine about the mind of the American corresponds to a historical political pattern, while most of what we have been able to determine about the Mexican mind corresponds to an interpersonal historical happening.

Let us begin the discussion of the historical political pattern of the United States with this statement: "We hold these truths to be self-evident, that all men are created equal, that they are endowed by their Creator with certain unalienable Rights, that among these are Life, Liberty, and the pursuit of Happiness."

This was, and still is, a wonderful statement. However, as a young American political scientist commented, it is a sadly incomplete statement. It certainly lacks a significant element of the French revolutionary slogan: liberty, equality, and *fraternity*.

The goals of liberty and equality, proclaimed by the highly individualistic people who left England seeking freedom of thought, led immediately to the creation of an American ideal: that every American could aspire to be president. Americans were to be individualistic, independent, competitive, self-initiated and self-reinforced, oriented toward achievement, efficient, and successful. Aided by socioeconomic events, this type of thinking flourished and produced a thriving economy. It soon became clear, however, that members of

[1] Mesonorthamerica is the only geographically and historically realistic name for "America."

some groups were not so easily becoming president as were members of other groups. The socioculture faced an alternative: either people are not equal, or some people do not take advantage of their opportunities. For a culture based on the ideal of equality it was easier to accept the second alternative. Other characteristics came into play, poverty and skin color, for example. The socioculture rationalized that those who did not take advantage of their equality were inferior, incapable, or lazy. In time it became evident, however, that the real problem was that these people did not have the same opportunities. The ideal of equality, with the same force as it had previously sustained one side of the question, now turned to the other and permitted the minorities to gain access to power. After all, the goals of freedom and equality imply that all individuals were originally endowed with the same amount of power. The United States of Mesonorthamerica is a "power-equality" socioculture in which affiliation, fraternity, and love, while not completely lacking, are not primary goals. It is this evident lack of fraternity, in the opinion of this writer, that has caused angry minorities to revolt and seek power. This apparent lack of love in the socioculture has caused youth to rebel and search for love and peace. But the original brutal force of the individualistic quest for power underlies even the extreme revolt of the "hippie," who professes peace and love but at the same time is determined to "do his own thing." In this socioculture power lies within the individual, while in the socialist sociocultures power lies primarily within the state and secondarily within the people as a whole.

On the other hand, a dramatic interpersonal interaction lies at the historical roots of the Mexican socioculture. Early in the sixteenth century, a few hundred Spaniards conquered a land inhabited, according to the historians, by eight million Indians. Its whole sociocultural historical background is based upon the union of a conqueror—the powerful, the male, the Spaniard—and the conquered—the female, the subjugated, the Indian. For a period of time it was believed that Indians had no souls but that children born to Spaniards and Indian women had them. I have jokingly remarked that it was undoubtedly a fervent religious zeal that led these few hundred Spaniards to put souls into the bodies of Indian women; this zeal created modern Mexico with its almost entirely mestizo population.

Sometime, somehow, consciously or unconsciously, this relationship crystallized into a decision that seems to hold the key to most dealings both within the Mexican family and within the Mexican socioculture. The decision was that all power was to be in the hands of the male and all love was to be in the hands of the female. Ever since, it appears, the male obtains the love of the female through a mythical mixture of power and love; any power the female acquires is by means of her loving behavior. As children grow up in this environment they see a mixture of power and love. It is my opinion that in Mexican interactions power and love are almost never completely separated from each other. One might say that there is not a significant differentiation between these two patterns of interpersonal interaction in the Mexican socioculture.

In the United States, where most people were confident that they were equal to anyone else, for a long time the system *ideally* treated them all equally (i.e., they all had equal rights under the law) but gave them different jobs in accordance with their cognitive ability and technical capacity. In Mexico, where all are theoretically *equal as far as affect* is concerned, power went to the loved ones. Thus in the Mexican socioculture power is bestowed, traditionally, upon those you love: your nuclear family, the extended family, your relatives, friends, etc. The American socioculture is the socioculture of power, and power is the main element in decision making. Mexico, on the other hand, is still a socioculture of love, and final decisions are made in terms more of affiliation than of power. It is within the warm network of affiliation that the Mexican grows into an interdependent, obedient individual. The Mexican socioculture, then, is an affiliative and hierarchical culture. In effect, power is primarily in the hands of the father; the mother also has power in terms of love and respect; and the rest are assumed to obey. As you will see in the cross-cultural studies of respect, there is a clear hierarchy of roles in Mexican society. The two extremes of the age continuum, the elderly and the very young, hold the highest status in the society. They are given respect, power, and love. Let us recall what is said about babies in Mexico: they are called *los reyes de la casa,* "the kings of the household." The elderly, the grandparents, who traditionally hold power over ultimate decisions, share this status.

Ultimately the historical traditional pattern of the United States will produce individuals who are *active* in the sense in which I define the term. They will be independent, individualistic, autonomous, oriented toward achievement, competitive, somewhat impulsive and aggressive, and rather tense and nervous. The Mexican historical-sociocultural pattern, on the other hand, will produce individuals who are obedient, affiliative, interdependent, orderly, cooperative, not oriented toward achievement, and not self-initiated.

However, our recent studies, particularly those carried out with children and adolescents in the late part of the sixties and early part of the seventies, indicate that both the American and the Mexican sociocultures are changing in direction. In some respects the urban Mexicans are moving toward traditional American cultural values, while Americans are moving toward a complex intermingling of strong affiliative and hedonistic elements with individualistic power and equality.

But let us return to the thoughts with which we prefaced our introduction to the two historical patterns. We mentioned the existence of at least two dimensions, the dimension of love and the dimension of power. Before going further let us define these concepts operationally. Love is any kind of behavior that will bring people closer, whether physically, emotionally, cognitively, socially, or spiritually. Thus the handshake, the *abrazo* or embrace, and the kiss are as much love as are cooperation, smiles, friendliness, affection, or more sophisticated behavior that enables others to be happy or happier, to develop their potentials, etc. Mexicans, the inventors of the warmest *abrazo*, specialize in this behavior. Power, on the other hand, is any kind of behavior by which we get others to do what we as individuals want to see done. This is the kind of behavior that puts ultimate decisions in our hands; it is often concerned more with ends than with means, although there is great interest in means as long as they are necessary to reach certain ends. In American society this power is equally allotted, in theory, to every individual, and Americans specialize in this kind of behavior. But, remember, we must consider the fact that both love and power can be efficacious or ineffi-cacious. I strongly believe that someday we shall be able to analyze the historical patterns of the Mesonorthamericans and of the Mexi-cans, not only in terms of power-equality and affiliation-hierarchy, but also in terms of the efficacy or inefficacy of these patterns for the life of individuals, couples, groups, and societies. The research al-ready done leads one to believe that, while the Mexican socioculture has been more efficacious in the area of mental health and interper-sonal relationships, the American socioculture has been far more effi-cacious in dealing with problems of power, equality, and, in partic-ular, economics. At this moment, when both sociocultures seem to be departing from their traditional historical patterns and moving in opposite directions, it is time to stop and consider the dimension of efficacy-inefficacy.

As you will see in several of the studies in this book, there is an-other important dimension measured in the attempt to differentiate the American from the Mexican socioculture. This is the active-pas-sive dimension. In some way still not clear to us, the power-equality socioculture of the United States has fostered an active way of facing the stress of life: whenever members of this culture face stress, they seem to feel that the way to resolve the problem, diminishing the stress, is to modify the environment, whether physical, interpersonal, or social. (Should we call this the exercise of individual power?)

The Mexican socioculture, on the other hand, has chosen a differ-ent method of resolving the problems set by the environment, the stresses faced by individual Mexicans. Mexicans seem to feel that the best way to resolve problems is to modify oneself rather than to mod-ify the physical, interpersonal, or social environment. (Should we call this the love motive?)

At any rate, we are confident that cross-cultural research will pro-vide us with a clearer idea of the ways in which power and love inter-act in human relations relative to the dimensions of efficacy-inefficacy and of active versus passive reactions to stress; then we shall be in a better position to develop some interesting directives in the areas of mental health, human development, and human understanding.

To end this long introduction, let us make one more schematic attempt to characterize the Anglo-American. Let us turn to his expectations and his views of life, as derived from his historical-socio-cultural process. We have found that for one reason or another he feels that life is to be enjoyed rather than endured. In view of the historical individualism aimed at accomplishment, we can see that throughout his history he has wanted to do "his own thing" (whatever he himself pleases—the full exercise of individual power); strangely, it was not until the advent of the hippies that he was able to express this desire clearly. He is equal to anyone else, but he has been told that he can be better than anyone else, and as a result he often tries to be *more equal* than the rest. I see the rise of women's liberation as a result of this incessant urge to be "more equal than thou." Historically the Anglo-American has wanted to be clean, neat, and socially acceptable; the beatniks and the hippies have rebelled against this notion. One of the greatest assets of the American historical socioculture has been the Anglo-American's desire for and intense pursuit of excellence in his individual achievement, the achievement motive discussed by David C. McClelland.[2] The beatniks and the hippies rebelled against this notion also and offered peace and love as a substitute. At the same time, however, there was a profound hedonistic trend, especially among the hippies—who unwittingly and vigorously promoted the values of the affluent society. They believed that life is to be enjoyed, no matter how, and that pleasure is an end in itself. This vision of American society as consisting of self-centered individuals in search of pleasure (and the pursuit of happiness?) is not a pleasing one; on the other hand, there is the beautiful urge for equality, perhaps more vigorous than ever, expressed in gigantic attempts to make the poor and the minorities equal, at least in opportunity, to the rest of society. Indeed, this is an admirable historical socioculture, whose greatest accomplishment has been to create the largest economic, industrial, and military power on the face of the earth, while doing its utmost to maintain freedom, particularly specific individual freedoms. Love has also existed but more often than not has been subjugated to power. It is here that the hippie revolu-

[2] David C. McClelland et al., *The Achievement Motive.*

tion reaches its highest point: it insists that love cannot exist unless it goes hand in hand with another dimension, peace.

The scheme for the Mexican is totally different: life is not to be enjoyed; it is to be endured. The Mexican expects life to be hard and demanding. But, as I have insisted many times, he ends by enjoying life, as a child, as a young man, and even as an adult, much more than the American child, youth, and adult ever seem to enjoy it. His notion of individual enjoyment and of individual power, however, is vague at best. If he were to say something similar to the hippies' slogan, he would cite "my own family thing" as the goal for his individual functioning. In the midst of a contrasting culture, it is possible to extend the notion of "my own family" to "my own race." Consider the phenomenon of *la raza unida*. Not "my own thing" but "my own *raza* thing." Thus the notions of individual power and of individual love are not as differentiated as they are in the Anglo-American historical tradition. Love subjugates power more often than not; but sometimes, unexpectedly and without differentiation, power surges up and becomes the possessor and even the tyrant of love. There is no sense of individual equality or of the search for individual power, but rather a defined hierarchical ordering of the individuals within the family: the father exercises power because he is respected; the mother exercises power because she is loved. The children have power because they love and are loved, because they are interdependent with their parents, and, particularly, because they are members of the main unit of power in Mexico: the family. Achievement is fundamentally affiliative; the idea of a standard of excellence against which to measure oneself is nebulous at best. Work is a labor of love, but it lacks the persistence and the constant check of reality that are found in the traditional American goal of achievement. Since the Mexican often resolves problems by changing himself rather than the environment, he knows many subtle ways of dealing with himself. He knows how to modify his emotions and his moods. On the other hand, he is quite incapable of anticipating the very many details that may go wrong when he acts in the physical and economic environments. It is the eternal story: at the last moment when a decision must be made, several details indispensable to a wise decision are lacking. The Mexican in fact feels that it is better to know how to obey than to command. It is true, however, that the new urban generations are somewhat different. Individual accomplishment is beginning to be rewarded; there is greater clarity about levels of excellence; a more active attitude toward events is being taken; and so on. The pattern of obedience, although still strong, is beginning to wane. At the same time there is a surge of the money-making motive. The future of the historical sociocultural pattern of the Mexican is still quite uncertain. The future for the Mexican-American lies in developing a second *mestizaje* or crossbreeding: he must embody the best of his two parent cultures. He must retain affiliation and love as fundamental goals while making sure that his love is not inefficacious but efficacious. This means that he must master technologies and put them to the service of his own people—until the *raza* begets equality of opportunity—and then to the service of all humanity.

R. Díaz-Guerrero

Psychology of the Mexican

CULTURE AND PERSONALITY

1. Neurosis and the Mexican Family Structure

In the following description of the Mexican family, I should like to make clear that only the dominant Mexican family pattern is described and that variants are only incidentally touched upon.[1]

The Mexican family is founded upon two fundamental propositions: (a) the unquestioned and absolute supremacy of the father and (b) the necessary and absolute self-sacrifice of the mother. The mother's role has from times unknown acquired an adequate qualifi-

NOTE. This essay was originally published in the *American Journal of Psychiatry*, vol. 112, 1955, pp. 411–417. Copyright 1955 the American Psychiatric Association.

[1] As may be seen from its use in this paper, the term *dominant pattern* is used here in a manner similar but not equivalent to that of F. R. Kluckhohn in "Dominant and Variant Value Orientations," in *Personality in Nature, Society and Culture*, ed. Clyde Kluckhohn, H. A. Murray, and D. F. Schneider. Gregory Bateson's "Cultural Determinants of Personality," in *Personality and the Behavior Disorders*, ed. J. McV. Hunt, and Clyde Kluckhohn's "Values and Value Orientations in the Theory of Action: An Exploration in Definition and Classification," in *Toward a General Theory of Action*, ed. Talcott Parsons and Edward A. Shils, have also influenced this writer.

cation in the term *abnegation,* which means the denial of any and all possible selfish aims.

These two fundamental propositions in the family derive from more general "existential" value orientations or, better, generalized sociocultural assumptions which imply an indubitable, biological, and natural superiority of the male. We shall try to demonstrate that the role playing of the members of the Mexican family follows closely—as conclusions follow premises—from the stated sociocultural propositions.

Even before a Mexican child is born, a set of expectations is already at work. Although in many societies there is a preference for boy babies, in Mexico the stress is greater—it *ought* to be a boy! The birth of a girl, unless she appears after one or two but preferably three boys, is somewhat of an emotional tragedy. In the past, more seriously, and recently, more jokingly, the virility of a father who gives birth to a girl is considered questionable. Besides this threat, the birth of a girl is undesirable for other reasons: (*a*) it means a bad economic break; (*b*) it imposes emotional and physical strain on the family that must compulsively guard her honor, which is equivalent to the family's honor (fundamentally, the loss of virginity in a female out of wedlock threatens brutally the fundamental premise of femininity and self-sacrifice in the female); (*c*) even the best solution through her marriage brings into the family a strange male intruder; (*d*) if she should not marry she will become a *cotorra,* literally, an "old female parrot," an individual with eternal neurotic complaints that are a burden to the family.

One may well ask: why a girl at all? However, after several boys, one girl is desirable in the sense that she will serve her brothers, thus allowing the wife more time to care maternally for the husband.

But let us see now the role expectations for the male child. Above all, he must grow up to fit the dignified role of a male. There must be no dolls or doll houses, but soldiers, guns, military helmets, broomstick horses, swords, titanic yells, imposing screams, panic among the little girls. Any little demonstration of feminine interests will be disapproved by older brothers, uncles, cousins, and the mother herself. Older children discriminate against younger ones on the basis that they are not sufficiently male (*machos*) to participate in their games, which become progressively more "masculine" (rougher but also implicating a certain dramatically conceded masculinity). Thus the younger children look forward with longing to the attainment of greater virility. Little girls are either avoided or a "steam-roller" attitude is taken toward them.

The female child must grow up to her destiny: superlative femininity, the home, maternity. The little girls amuse themselves with dolls and "playing house." They must stay away from the rough games of the boys, for, as the educated people explain, it would not be ladylike to participate in them. This idea is based apparently on variants of the widespread belief that if a girl should run or jump she would become a man. Very early the little girl starts helping her mother in the home chores—an area tabooed for the male child. In order to acquire greater femininity the little girl must start learning delicate feminine activities like embroidery or lace making. Later in life she may learn painting, music, poetry, literature, or philosophy. But even as a little girl she must always dress like a female, keep neat, and be graceful and coquettish. It is interesting to note that one of the postulates under which Mexican public education has labored for years is that one of the main goals of education is to make men more typically male and women more typically female.

During the entire childhood the sign of virility in the male is courage to the point of temerity, aggressiveness, and not to run away from a fight or break a deal (*no rajarse*). But both the boy and the girl must be obedient within the family. Paradoxically, a father will feel proud of the child who did not run from a fight in the street but at home may punish him severely for having disobeyed his orders regarding street fights. This appears to mean that the child must be masculine, but not as much so as his father.

During adolescence the sign of virility in the male is to talk about or act in the sexual sphere. He who possesses information and/or experience regarding sexual matters is inevitably the leader of the group. The prepubescent boys are coldly discriminated from the

albures[2] sessions of adolescents on the basis that they are not sufficiently masculine to participate. Girls, instead of being avoided, are
now the alluring goal of the males. During adolescence there comes
into being a peculiar phenomenon. The pursuit of the female unfolds
into two aspects. In one the adolescent searches for the ideal woman
—the one he would like to convert into his wife. This one must have
all the attributes of the perfect feminine role. She must be chaste,
delicate, homey (*hogareña*), sweet, maternal, dreamy, religious, and
must not smoke or cross her legs. Her face must be beautiful, especially her eyes—but not necessarily her body. Sexuality takes a very
secondary role. In the other aspect the adolescent searches for the
sexualized female with the clear purpose in mind of sexual inter-
course. Here the roundness of the lines and their quantity are determinant factors. The male Mexican's female ideal implies breasts
and hips, particularly hips, far broader and far more quivering than is
considered proper in the United States. It is even more interesting to
note that in every case as soon as the individual has found the woman
he may idealize, ipso facto, all other women become objects for the
sexualized search and tempting objects of seduction.

As adolescence advances into youth and adulthood, the extreme
differentiation among feminine objects loses some of its momentum.
And, although the entire expression of sexuality is still only open to
lovers or prostitutes, it is also true that the youth or the adult who
looks for a woman with matrimonial intentions will, before making
his decisions, attend a little more to the quality and quantity of the
secondary sexual characteristics of the female. It is well to repeat,
however, that even in this case chastity and the other factors of femininity continue to weigh heavily.

From adolescence on, through the entire life of the male, virility
will be measured by the sexual potential, and only secondarily in
terms of physical strength, courage, or audacity. So much so, that
even these other characteristics of behavior, as well as still other
subtler ones, are believed to be dependent upon the sexual capacity.
The accent falls upon the sexual organs and their functions. The size

[2] *Albures*: words with a sexual double sense.

of the penis has its importance. The size of the testicles has more, but more important than the physical size is the "functional" size. It is assumed they are functioning well when (a) the individual acts efficiently in sexual activity or speaks or brags convincingly of his multiple seductive successes; (b) he speaks or actually shows that he is not afraid of death; (c) he is very successful in the fields of intellectuality, science, etc.

In each of these cases the common people, those that Samuel Ramos speaks of as putting things crudely,[3] will say, "That guy has plenty of nuts (*muchos huevos*)!"—or else that he has them very well placed. This sociocultural proposition of profound depth and breadth seems to embrace in its scope the majority of the Latin American people. A Cuban physician once told me how one of the Cuban presidents had gone alone into a large military post where the commanding general was preparing a coup d'état. Man to man, the president made the general confess and made him a prisoner of his former followers. The Cuban physician summed up the story by saying, "Oh! What a man; his testicles are bigger than a cathedral." It is not only the monumental size attributed to the testicles that is amazing in this remark, but also the inclusion in one sentence of the two opposing sociocultural premises: the testicles, virility; the cathedral, the female set of values.

Finally, even the undisputed authority of the male in the home and in all other functions in relation to the female may be explained by the fact that he has testicles and she does not. Incidents like the following are very common among university students: if one of Mexico's relatively few career women obtains high grades, one or many of the male students will exert himself to express with a serious face and in a loud whisper that he knows from reliable sources that this student has already missed several menstruations. Americans would leap to the conclusion that the girl is pregnant, but in Mexico the implication is that she is becoming a male.

Let us return to the female. After the termination of the grade school, she is returned to the home. It is not feminine to have an ad-

[3] Samuel Ramos, *El perfil del hombre y la cultura en México*.

vanced education. During adolescence women learn more and more
the varied aspects of their roles. Now substituting for, now helping
the mother in her care and attentions to the males, she irons, washes,
cooks, sews buttons, purchases socks and undershorts for her brothers (I was twenty-five and in the United States before I bought my
own underclothes), and is supposed to fulfill the most menial needs
of her brothers. The brothers in turn are the faithful custodians of
the chastity of the female. On the basis that nothing can happen to
the sister if there are no male strangers around, even innocent court-
ships, where well-intentioned gentlemen talk through the railings of
a window with girls, are viewed with suspicion. As a consequence,
these gentlemen are the objects of hostility and are seen from the
corner of the eye, and the family batteries are ready to shoot in case
that such a boy friend may dare to hold the hand of the sister. The
precautions are taken to such an extreme that often the friends of the
father or brothers are never admitted into the homes—except of
course if there is a fiesta, at which time there is a breaking down of
most premises. At any rate, it is in this fashion that the girl is prepared to give and give—and receive little or nothing. But it is during
adolescence and youth that the Mexican women are going to experience their happiest period. In effect, they will sooner or later be
converted into the ideal woman for a given male. Then they will be
placed on a pedestal and be highly overevaluated. The girl in this
period will receive poems, songs, gallantries, serenades, and all the
tenderness of which the Mexican male is capable. Such tokens are
numerous, for the male has learned very well in his infancy, through
his relations with his mother, a very intensive and extensive reper-
toire for the expression of affection; and, as a part of the maternal
ideals, romanticism and idealism dig deep into the mental structure
of the Mexican. At any rate, our Cinderella, who has heretofore
given all and received nothing in exchange, enters into an ecstatic
state as a result of this veneration, this incredible submission—as a
slave to a queen—of the imposing, proud, dictatorial, and conceited
male. Many years later the Mexican female will again experience an
ecstasy of the same quality when her children will consider her the
dearest being in existence. But this is not surprising—both expres-

sions of sentimentality are only branchings of the same fundamental phenomenon: the set of maternal values.

Soon after the termination of the honeymoon, the husband passes from slave to master and the woman enters the hardest test of her life. The idealism of the male rapidly drops away toward the mother. To make matters worse, the wife cannot be considered as a sexual object in a broad sense. Mexican husbands repeatedly indicate that sex must be practiced in one way with the wife and in another with the lover. The most common statement refers to the fear that the wife might become too interested in sex if he introduced her to the subtleties of the pleasure. At other times this fear is expressed in a clearer fashion by saying that the wife might become a prostitute.

The husband must work and provide. He knows nothing, nor does he want to know anything, about what happens in the home. He demands only that all obey him and that his authority be unquestioned. Often, after working hours, he joins his friends and along with them proceeds with a life no different from that he practiced when unmarried. Toward his children he shows affection but, before anything else, authority. Although he doesn't follow them himself, he demands adherence to the "maternal" religious concepts. Often, however, he imposes the authority of his moods and his whims. He is satisfied if his children obey, "right or crooked." It is therefore again the premise of unquestioned authority. The wife submits and, deprived of the previous idealization, must serve him to his satisfaction "the way mother did." Since this is not possible, the husband often becomes cruel and brutal toward the wife.

The Mexican wife enters much before motherhood in the causeway of abnegation—the denial of all her needs, and the absolute pursuit of the satisfaction of everyone else.

In this frame of reference, we shall describe the aspect that is lacking—the infancy of the Mexican. The Mexican mother is deeply affectionate and tender and overprotective toward the infant. In the beginning the baby gets anything and everything. Infants are deeply loved, fondled, and admired—for the first two years of their existence. In this activity the usually large number of relatives participate. At the same time, slowly in the first two years and then under an intensive pressure, the infant and the child must become well brought up, *bien educado*. They must become the model children who will perforce fit into the system of absolute obedience to the parents. This necessary obedience, humility, and respect to the elders and for authority are imposed in a great many ways. Drilling in courtesy and in manners is a prevalent one. Thus, a well-brought-up child may not yet be able to pronounce his name properly, but when asked what it is he must invariably follow his answer with *"para servirle"* or *"a sus ordenes"* ("to serve you" or "at your orders"). The Spanish language is saturated with these forms of submission. Actually there are two languages, and when two people meet the one in the position of submission refers to the other as *usted*; the one in the position of command uses *tu*, a familiar form for "you."

The infant must be well brought up, and if words do not suffice, as they often do not, physical punishment is used. The child must learn submission and obedience. In the same fashion he learns in a rigid way the various aspects of the Catholic religion. To end this description, let us say that the mother, with her attitude and her affect, is the source of all tenderness, sentimentality—and the largest portion of the cultural expressions of the Mexican. The writing, painting, sculpture, philosophy, and religion are saturated with direct or symbolic allusions to maternity.

In spite of the fact that this is a summarized and incomplete elaboration of the Mexican family pattern, one can easily conclude that the general setting is favorable to the development of neurosis. Also, one is prone to think that the Mexican female would be commonly subject to neurosis. Table 1-1 seems to substantiate such predictions: 32% (± 2.65%) of the male population of Mexico City over 18 years of age is "neurotic" and 44% (± 2.83%) of the female population over 18 is "neurotic." The difference is statistically significant to the 0.4% level of confidence.

At a more specific level one can easily deduce that in the male there should be (*a*) problems of submission, conflict, and rebellion in the area of authority; (*b*) preoccupation and anxiety regarding sexual potency; (*c*) conflict and ambivalence regarding his double role: he must at times love and generally act maternally and tenderly,

Table 1-1
Degree of Mental Health

	Men			Women		
	Yes	No	Don't Know	Yes	No	Don't Know
1. Are you happier alone than in company?	(12)	82	0	(26)	66	8
2. Do you get angry frequently?	(43)	56	1	(62)	36	2
3. Do you think life is worth living?	77	(12)	11	69	(18)	13
4. Are you a nervous person?	(43)	52	5	(66)	33	1
5. Do you take offense easily?	(43)	51	6	(51)	40	9
6. Do you often feel very depressed?	(34)	64	2	(57)	41	2
7. Do you like the type of work with which you earn your living?	68	(27)	5	80	(9)	11
8. Do you get along better with friends than with members of your family?	(29)	66	5	(37)	59	4
9. Do you believe in trusting people?	27	(63)	10	13	(77)	10
10. Do you find it difficult to concentrate on what you read or study?	(21)	68	11	(24)	58	18
11. Do you suffer frequently from bile?[a]	(28)	66	6	(52)	47	1

SOURCE: Data are taken from the study described in Essay 4.

"Neurosis" is defined by the type of answers enclosed in parentheses.

[a] "Bile" refers to the Mexican tradition that, when a person is badly or cruelly frustrated, bile will pour into the blood and produce all kinds of strange symptoms: abdominal pains, vomiting, diarrhea, headaches, dizziness, oppression, migraine, etc. Most of the disorders now called psychophysiological can be produced.

and at other times act sexually and virilely; (d) difficulties in superseding the maternal stage: dependent-feminine individuals; (e) problems before and during marriage: mother's love interferes with the love to another woman (here one should expect an important area of stress where the husband, the wife, and the husband's mother play the dynamics of jealousy); (f) the Oedipus complex, as Freud describes it: almost every aspect of the ideal setting for its development is provided by the premises of the culture and the role playing. Actually areas b, c, d, and e above may be considered as partial expressions of the dynamics of the Oedipus complex.

In the female the main area of stress should fall around her variable success in living up to the stiff requirements that the cultural

premises demand. Her inability to live up to them should show itself
in self-belittlement and depressive trends. Another area of clear
disturbance should appear around the "old maid" complex. Finally,
the rapid transition of the sociocultural premises may affect her.

Interestingly enough, even the occasional observer has opportunity
to see evidences of mental ill health in the areas outlined above for
the male. My own observation in the practice of psychotherapy has,
in many instances, substantiated the expectation that these areas are
the most stress producing. In regard to women there is little evidence. Women in Mexico seldom go to the psychiatrist. It is a common observation, however, that more women than men go to the
general practitioner with psychosomatic ailments. Table 1-1 shows
that the question dealing with depressive mood is differentially answered in the affirmative by the females, and the only (and very
carefully selected) question regarding psychosomatic ailments, "Do
you suffer frequently from bile?" shows twice as many women as
men suffering from it.

But what seems to be even more commonplace in one degree or
another is the existence in the Mexican male of a syndrome for which
the common denominator is guilt. The extreme separation between
the "female set" of values and the "male set," plus the fact that it is the
female who teaches and develops the personality of the child, often
provokes in the male guilt regarding deviations from the female pattern. Actually, in order to be at ease with the male pattern he must
constantly break with the female one. Perhaps it is not an accident
that the main religious symbol is a woman: the Virgin of Guadalupe.
From their behavior it appears that the males are caught in a com-
pulsive asking for forgiveness from the same symbol they must betray
if they are to be masculine. It is only because a good number succeed
in keeping each role distinct and separate, through clear discrimination of the places and situations suitable for the playing of each,
that no more or no more serious mental disturbance appears. In many
of the male Mexican patients that I have seen there is, to one degree
or another, prominent in the picture a battle of "superego" and "id,"
the former representing the mother set of values and the latter the
father set. This is Freudian, metapsychology à la mexicaine.

Table 1-2
Sociocultural Premises (Values)

	Men			Women		
	Yes	No	Don't Know	Yes	No	Don't Know
1. Is the mother for you the dearest person in existence?	95	3	2	86	10	4
2. Do you believe that woman's place is in the home?	91	6	3	90	7	3
3. Do you believe that men should "wear the pants in the family"?	85	11	4	78	15	7
4. Do you think that many of your desires are contrary to your moral and religious ideas?	—	—	—	19	72	9
5. Do you believe it is proper for women to go out alone with men?	56	35	9	55	34	11
6. Do you believe that men are more intelligent than women?	44	44	12	23	60	17
7. Do you believe that the stricter the parents are, the better the children turn out?	41	44	15	40	55	5
8. Do you think that most married men have mistresses?	51	33	16	63	17	20
9. Do you think it is natural for married men to have mistresses?	22	67	11	16	74	10
10. If you are a woman do you consider yourself very feminine?	—	—	—	54	35	11

SOURCE: Data are taken from the study described in Essay 4.
The answer "yes" corresponds to the dominant pattern except in questions 4 and 5, where "no" corresponds to the dominant pattern.

From this vantage point one could say that many of the neurosis-provoking conflicts in the Mexican are "inner" conflicts, that is, provoked more by clashes of values than by clashes of the individual with reality. That this may be so is further suggested by a study of José Gómez Robleda.[4] Searching for the evaluations of the "average Mexican" he found that 34.34% of the people investigated held as their main interest in life "sexuality and eroticism" and 17.17%, mystical and religious values.

[4] José Gómez Robleda, *Imagen del mexicano*.

The data in Table 1-2 seem to substantiate the masculine-feminine sociocultural dichotomy. The table is self-explanatory in the context of the statements about the main sociocultural premises. With more adequate polling techniques, one could measure the degree and perhaps the "quality" of the variation from the dominant patterns. For example, there is still little variation in regard to the cultural assumption "The mother is the dearest person in existence," but there is a tremendous change in regard to "Men are more intelligent than women."

Summary

A presentation is made of the cultural assumptions which it is believed underlie a great deal of the role playing in the Mexican family. Examples are given to demonstrate the effect of the assumptions in actual role playing. Remarks are made regarding (a) the areas where neurotic difficulty would be expected from the assumptions and the role playing and (b) some evidence which seems to verify such expectations. It is proposed that opinion polls may serve the purpose of identifying the degree of variation of a given group from the dominant pattern.

Commentaries on the First Study

This study was read in May of 1955 during one of the sessions of the Annual Congress of the American Psychiatric Association. The study provoked much discussion among those attending. Among those present were some Latin American psychiatrists. It is interesting to note that the Latin Americans, with the exception of a Peruvian, observed that the panorama described in the paper was completely applicable to the families in their particular countries. Subsequently, Drs. E. D. Maldonado Sierra, R. Fernández Marina, and Richard D. Trent, all of the Puerto Rican Institute of Psychiatry, showed intense interest in the study and in the original questionnaire, especially in the part of the questionnaire dealing with the sociocultural premises of the Mexican family. Dr. Trent, with our permission, prepared a questionnaire of 123 statements, including the ten based on the original scale of sociocultural premises. His questionnaire not only amplifies the original but also observes all the precautions advised by modern statistical techniques to ensure the reliability of the results. The primary interest of the Puerto Rican doctors was to submit their questionnaire to a sample of Puerto Ricans and compare their results with those we obtained from our study.

The results of the doctors' study appeared in early 1958 in volume 48, pages 167–181, of the *Journal of Social Psychology*, under the title "Three Basic Themes in Mexican and Puerto Rican Family Values." After mentioning extensive bibliographic references to the psychological similarities existing among the various Latin American countries, they present the results obtained from submitting the questionnaire to 521 students of both sexes at the University of Puerto Rico. (Answers were obtained from 494 of these.) In Table 1-3 we compare the results obtained from the eight questions that were equivalent in the two questionnaires. Despite the fact that our study was based on a more or less representative sample of the population of Mexico City over eighteen years of age, while the Puerto Rican sample was drawn from university students, the degree of similarity in the results is almost incredible. The Puerto Rican study amplifies our knowledge of the psychology of the Latin American family, and we recommend it to all interested in these questions.

Although, as we stated in the prologue, the fundamental purpose of the study of the Mexican family was to discover the factors within it that tend to provoke conflict and frustration and therefore neurosis, we should point out once more that there are positive values within the family that exercise effective force, although they are not considered in this study. For example, the traditional cohesiveness and closeness of the members of the Mexican family seem to be definite factors in preventing juvenile delinquency. Along with Dr. Abraham Maslow, we have discussed various positive aspects of the Mexican family in an article titled "Delinquency as a Value Disturbance," which we published jointly as one of the chapters of the book *Festschrift for Gardner Murphy*, issued by Harper Brother in 1961.

Table 1-3

Percentage of Affirmative Responses of Mexicans and Puerto Ricans
to Questions Related to Sociocultural Premises

Mexicans (294 participants)

Stimulus	Men (%)	Women (%)
1. Is the mother for you the dearest person in existence?	95	86
2. Do you believe that woman's place is in the home?	91	90
3. Do you believe that men should "wear the pants in the family"?	85	78
4. Do you believe that the stricter the parents are, the better the children turn out?	41	40
5. Do you believe that men are more intelligent than women?	44	23
6. Do you think that most married men have mistresses?	51	63
7. Do you think it is natural for married men to have mistresses?	22	16
8. Do you believe it is proper for women to go out alone with men?	35	34

Puerto Ricans (494 participants)

Stimulus	Men (%)	Women (%)
1. For me the mother is the dearest person in the world.	84	89
2. Woman's place is in the home.	81	77
3. The man should wear the pants in the family.	81	65
4. The stricter the parents are, the better the child will be.	12	6
5. Men are more intelligent than women.	64	16
6. Most married men have mistresses.	36	42
7. It is natural for married men to have mistresses.	25	7
8. It is appropriate for a woman to go out alone with men.	25	7

SOURCE: The Puerto Rican statistics are from the work by Fernández Marina, Maldonado Sierra, and Trent mentioned in the text. The stimuli in this study were statements or affirmations rather than questions. The subjects placed an X by the affirmation with which they agreed and left the others blank. As indicated in the text, the questionnaire included 123 stimuli.

2. Mexican Assumptions about
Interpersonal Relations

It is amazing how often psychotherapists will say to their patients, "The main problem is that you do not face reality." This statement of the patient's problem would seem simple and self-evident. The unspoken assumption, however, is that there is a "reality" that everyone can get to know and that the task of psychotherapy is to help the patient first to see, then to face this "reality."

Underlying this assumption is the familiar Western concept of an objective, concrete reality "out there." Undoubtedly this reality is an important one for us all to recognize. But is there not another kind of reality that must be accounted for? I refer to the reality created by the interactions between two or more people in a social or communicative relationship—their attitudes toward each other, their expectations of each other, the many intangibles, conscious and unconscious, of their mutual feelings. This "interpersonal reality," as I should like to call it, may be more important in human relations than the external reality.

NOTE. This essay was originally published in *ETC.: A Review of General Semantics* 16, no. 2 (Winter 1959), pp. 185–188.

Let us distinguish then between two kinds of reality: the *external* physical reality—the reality of nature; and the *interpersonal* reality of a state of affairs between two or more persons.

Let me select some examples of this interpersonal reality drawn from comparisons between Mexican and American cultures. There are some fundamental differences between the sociocultural assumptions of the complex Spanish-Mestizo-Indian grouping that constitutes the Mexican nationality and those of the Anglo-Saxon, Western European–derived culture of the United States.

Americans tend to view external reality as something to be subjected to their will, and the success of American technology is evidence of this orientation. Latin Americans, however, take a more fatalistic attitude toward nature and feel subjugated by it. Traditionally, Mexicans have done little to put external reality under their control.

However, Mexicans tend surprisingly to assume that interpersonal reality can be modified at will. Interpersonal reality is not just a given state of affairs, as it is so often to Americans ("The neighbors *are* unfriendly," "Mr. Jones *is* a snob," etc.). It is highly fluid, because *I* am there and am able to act upon it. The most important implication of this assumption is that people actually *create* salient qualities of this interpersonal reality.

Here is another basic Mexican assumption. An interpersonal reaction is evaluated on the basis of the immediate pleasure and satisfaction it brings. By this I do not mean getting bridges built or even getting a job, but providing human rapport for the people involved.

Ask a Mexican for street directions. He will often go into a complex series of explanations and gestures, frequently grinning; he will make you *feel* good. But you may get nowhere with his directions! Simply because he cannot answer your question, the Mexican would never let the *real thing*, the pleasant interpersonal encounter, go to waste. A definition of such a concept of interpersonal reality as found among Mexicans might go like this: "The degree of reality of an interpersonal situation lies in the frequency, quality, and warmth of the interpersonal reactions that can be achieved in a given period of time." Such reactions are spontaneous and are more like choices than conventional responses. Even when conventionally worded, these reactions are not stereotyped but have varied and pleasing emotional content.

The marketplace of the Aztecs was far more a place to socialize than a place to trade. This tradition continues today. The Indian woman spreads her pottery in the street: two dozen cups and plates. The tourist likes the price and asks for the whole lot. To the tourist's surprise, the woman says in horror, "No! If you take them all what will I have to sell?" The process, the ceremony, the socialization of selling are to her far more important than the sale—much as she and her children could use the money.

Mexicans have thus developed some exquisite ways of relating to one another: politeness, *buena educación*, friendliness, romanticism, etc. Although Mexican social gestures have been criticized as mere formalities, to me they seem to be as honest as anything a person can show. Perhaps Mexicans have gone too far in this way of thinking; they would rather lose an argument than lose a friend. Americans, of course, win the arguments. But Mexicans will lose not only arguments but time and money as well so as not to lose interpersonal fun.

This concept of interpersonal reality is extremely suggestive for marital relations. Here the degree of "truth" in statements made between man and wife should be measured not in terms of their correspondence to external reality but in terms of how well they help the couple get along. The verbal interchanges in marriage are not to be evaluated in terms of map-territory relationships, as if they were statements made at a conference of physicists, but rather in terms of their utility in creating and re-creating the on-going relationship.[1] This is not to advocate a complete break with external reality, but to say that there is something more important than being objectively "right" in domestic controversies.

Psychoanalytic schools in the United States consider their systems to be dynamic. Yet in practice, since they hold to the view that reality is something that must be "faced" and fail to distinguish interper-

[1] The expression *map-territory relationship*, frequently used in writings on general semantics, refers to the relationship between affirmations (the "map") and demonstrable facts (the "territory").

sonal from external reality, they hold to an extremely static view of human relations. They often hold to an elaborate but rigidly set view of what interpersonal relations are. That is, a boy "cannot" escape hating his father, "cannot" escape wanting to eliminate him, "cannot" escape desiring the mother libidinally, "cannot" escape being jealous of his brother or sister. Parents are helpless to modify the situation; the interpersonal relations are set. Even Harry Stack Sullivan, of the "interpersonal theory" of psychiatry, prefers—more flexibly, however —to have interpersonal relations defined and done with on the basis of avoidance of anxiety.

Furthermore, in their demand upon patients to "face reality," American psychiatrists often assume that this must inevitably be an unpleasant task for the patient—that to see what's what is to see something grim, dark, forbidding. Mexicans will not readily concede that reality—especially interpersonal reality—is necessarily forbidding. Hence in the psychotherapeutic situation a Mexican would see no a priori reason why it should not include a good deal of levity, light-heartedness, and humor.

Psychotherapists have generally recognized *within* the individual the strong sense of one's own identity that is often called "the *to-me* feeling." There can be a similar feeling *between* individuals, which might be called "the enjoying-each-other feeling." There is a deeper kind of "togetherness" than that now being exploited in some American advertising.

The "togetherness" of interpersonal reality is so important, especially in the psychotherapeutic situation, that other realities have no meaning or consequence until the persons or groups involved have developed a reasonably fluid and friendly relationship and created their own interpersonal reality. If, as here proposed, learning in interpersonal situations is dependent upon our ability to get along, we can see the need to explore further the "together feeling" so highly valued in Latin American cultures.

3. Motivations of the Mexican Worker

I am very glad to be among you, and I hope that I can tell you some things and listen to you in return, so that we all learn something about this problem, one which has been almost virgin territory until now: the problem of the motivation of the Mexican worker. In several ways this meeting has its historical aspects; it is very probable that this is the first time in Mexican history that a group like this one, with a psychologist and a group of executives, has sat down to discuss the behavior of the Mexican worker in relation to his work. It is the more historic because the approach is specifically psychological and, as Señor Campbell[1] said, has to do not with the more or less superficial aspects of behavior but rather with deep-seated causes, causes that are much more persistent and more intensely related to individual activity. What we could do first is examine some of the Mexican's expressions related to work. These expressions are not

NOTE. This essay was given as a lecture in the Instituto Mexicano de Administración de Negocios (IMAN), A.C., April 16, 1959. It has been translated by Cecile C. Wiseman.

[1] Donald Campbell, director of IMAN.

particularly optimistic in that they do not reveal strong motivation to work among Mexicans. You have probably heard them many times, but in light of our present concern you will find perhaps that they resonate with greater intensity.

We Mexicans say that "Work brutalizes," parodying the original expression that "Work ennobles." We say, "Idleness is the mother of the good life," instead of saying that "Idleness is the mother of all vices." Mexicans comment among themselves that the first thing is to make money in this life and then to retire "to scratch your belly." We often say that "Music that is paid for sounds bad." Other times we quote, "Don't work for free even for your father." In this series of expressions we find what is thought about work, at least on the level of superficial common sense. If we were to take these expressions seriously, we would close this conference immediately and say that nothing can be done, that we are stymied, that there is no way to motivate the Mexican to work. But in how many of these sayings is the Mexican expressing himself seriously? One should not forget that the Mexican has a great sense of humor; also it is quite likely that with this series of expressions he is referring to the more difficult aspects of work. I believe that the Mexican at work is rarely understood. If this is true, if the motivations of the working Mexican are not understood, it is likely that he will feel disturbed, hopeless, perhaps humiliated, and that then he will naturally not have much to offer in his work.

Let us start from the hypothesis that the expressions against work do not refer to work in itself, but rather to the conditions of work, especially in the past, but also in present-day Mexico. Some years ago I had the opportunity to carry out a study in which we asked a series of questions of a representative sample of the population of Mexico City.[2] One of the questions was "Do you like the type of work with which you earn your living?" Sixty-eight percent of the male population of Mexico City responded that they did like the type of work with which they earned their living, 27 percent responded that they did not, and 5 percent said that they did not know.

[2] See Essay 4.

Of course a negative response of 27 percent means that more than one in four thinks that way, and this constitutes a problem; but, in any case, the statements that "Idleness is the mother of the good life," and so on, do not seem to have such a decided and definite foundation if 68 percent do like the work with which they earn their living. At the very least we see then that there is a certain contradiction. The fact that this contradiction exists tells us that there should be something more, that we should investigate the situation more. We could not in truth leave this conference saying that the Mexican hates work—and add later that 68 percent of the male inhabitants of Mexico City over eighteen years old say that they like the work with which they earn their living. Let us explore this situation in greater depth.

In the first place, we need to have an idea of what motivation is, or what we mean by the motivation of behavior. We all know that an enormous number of different needs move human beings to action. In addition, you all know, since some of you have read it in Freud, Adler, Jung, Horney, etc., and others have heard it, that each of these authors claims that there is a fundamental need in the human being that in itself explains his mode of behavior. In reality, of course, there is no real contradiction. None of these authors is mistaken, but each one seems to concede greatest importance to only one of the multiple human needs. Recent psychology is becoming more and more aware that the motivation of human conduct is multiple and does not depend on any unique and exclusive need. Thus, the term *human motivation* refers to the forces, motives, needs, desires, instincts, impulses—whatever you wish to call them—concerned with the actions of human beings: with what they do, with what they do not do, and with what they prefer to do, etc. Therefore, if we are going to analyze the motivation of the Mexican worker, we must have a general but coherent idea of the fundamental, basic human needs, in accordance with the most recent and valid psychological findings.

We have said that in recent years the most accepted idea has been that of the plurality of the motives or impulses of human conduct. This pluralism has been supported by the most distinguished North American psychologists: Gordon W. Allport, Gardner Murphy,

Abraham H. Maslow, etc. I myself have also supported this idea and some time ago published an essentially similar concept here in Mexico.[3] Nevertheless, I believe that until now no one has been as clear, coherent, and thorough concerning this pluralistic attitude toward human motivation as Maslow. Here we will make use of the essence of his ideas relevant to the topic, taken from a publication of his in which he expresses them with great simplicity.[4]

Maslow says that before all else there exists a group of physiological needs. This is so obvious that no one would dispute it. For example, humans need to eat; we need water (I don't say "to drink" because the expression could be misunderstood); we need to sleep; we need to protect our bodies from extremes of temperature; we need, as well, to maintain a constant internal environment in the liquids that bathe our viscera. In blood, for example, the quantities of sugar, proteins, salts, etc., must be kept constant with only small variations. Fortunately, in this type of need we do not have to intervene voluntarily, since there are pre-established physiological mechanisms that maintain these internal constants, when and if the body is in a state of health, and there is an adequate opportunity to obtain, from external resources, the substances necessary to sustain this equilibrium. These physiological needs of man are indeed the most powerful. Fortunately, in this group at least, such needs have little effect on human behavior; that is to say, they are reasonably satisfied. But we know through recent historical events that, when hunger, for example, is not satisfied, it can develop brutal force and completely obscure all other needs, becoming the motivating impulse of greatest importance. A starving man would care little about tenderness, love, preservation of self-esteem, dignity, etc.; an insult would hardly matter to him, and he would even accept it gladly in exchange for a crust of bread. These last lines demand a further clarification of Maslow's organismic-pluralistic and dynamic theory of motivation.

This author tells us not only that the needs that explain human conduct are various but also that there are certain relationships

    [3] Rogelio Díaz Guerrero, "Ensayos de psicología dinámica y científica," Filosofía y Letras 25, nos. 49–50 (1953): 97–150.

    [4] Abraham H. Maslow, Motivation and Personality.

among them, a certain organization or integration. The fundamental principles that govern this organization of impulses are as follows: (*a*) There is a hierarchical organization in relation to the intensity of needs. The most intense ones are the physiological, followed by the rest in the order explained below. (*b*) When a group of needs is satisfied, it no longer affects motivation of behavior. The next group of needs in the hierarchical order becomes the preponderant one and in turn will motivate behavior until it is satisfied. (*c*) Thus, when various basic groups of human needs are satisfied, more subtle needs appear and develop in all their splendor.

Continuing with the group of physiological needs, we cannot overlook the sexual need. This need, which has an undeniable biological base, is nevertheless very complex in man and carries with it certain learned or cultural aspects.

A second group of human needs is that of preservation. This is simply the preservation of life in its various aspects. Let us call it the conservation of the integrity of the person as a biological being. Fundamentally these needs have great importance among children, as we all know. Children naturally need parental protection to a high degree. To them the environment appears constantly full of threatening situations that are unfamiliar to them and far beyond their physical and psychical capacities. We, the adults of a more or less civilized group, do not have these needs of personal safety so much on the surface; rather they are now more or less recognized and sufficiently satisfied. There are hospitals, doctors, antibiotics, vaccines, and a great number of other things that allow us to forget the question of mere physical survival. In addition, during our protected infancy and during adolescence, we have learned to dominate many fears.

Next there is another series of human needs. They are those of affection, tenderness, love; those of belonging, let us say, to a group of friends; those of belonging to large groups, institutions, etc. And these affiliative needs attain full development when the earlier ones in the hierarchy are sufficiently fulfilled. In that case, the latter needs assume the quality of most powerful, most fundamental, in a given moment for a specific human being. As you know, Erich Fromm attributes great importance to several of these needs. But once again we should remember and recognize that, even though it is certain that these are great human necessities, they lose their preponderance once they are duly satisfied. On the other hand, one can easily agree with Fromm in those cases in which individuals have really been completely deprived of affection all their lives. In such cases the need to obtain affection or love would be tremendously strong and could even provoke exaggerated neurotic attitudes aimed at satisfying it. But the most interesting thing is that perhaps here, in this Mexican group, mention of these needs of affection, tenderness, and love does not produce much impression or very strong reaction. This is due to the fact that, though the Mexican may have lacked many other things, he did not lack tenderness, affection, and love in his infancy. I believe that in many of these aspects Mexicans are sufficiently satisfied. Of course we delight in hearing about love and seeing it given great importance—but not as poor wretches starving for this sentiment. Rather, we approach it with the gusto of connoisseurs who can appreciate not only its existence but also the creative forms and manners of its refinement. Here, of course, the aesthetic and cognitive needs of which we shall speak later come into play. In any case, we have the impression that, in this aspect of love, Mexicans could turn out to be superior in various respects—which we shall analyze one day—to other groups of human beings. But there is something perhaps even more interesting: The Mexican should also be satisfied in relation to the need for friendship, the need for friends. In reality it seems that we are not satisfied. If we begin with simple, direct observation, it seems that the need to have friends is uncommonly intense in the Mexican; all our lives we are searching for friends; we constantly delight in coteries, parties, gossip, disputes, and all that sort of thing. This even provokes problems; as executives you probably complain, and your bosses probably do too, of this never-ending formation of coteries. In my experience as a customer in the large stores, I have observed now and again, frequently as victim, that the salesgirls stay in these groups instead of attending to the customers. This incessant talking seems to be a profound need of the Mexican; despite the fact that this talk, talk, talk goes on in the Mexican family, goes on at work, in the cafés, and everywhere, there is always talk and more talk with endless friends. This need ought to be filled to the brim; nevertheless, there it is, constant, obvious. There must be some reason for it; we shall investigate later to try to comprehend it.

After these needs, other very important ones follow in order; I refer to the needs to maintain or preserve self-esteem, in two aspects at least. One is that of being able to evaluate oneself with a certain stability and more or less positively; that is, to consider oneself as valuable. The other one is the need to be highly valued by others. This group of needs for self-esteem is very important in several ways. Hence we shall explore it at some length, because, as we shall see later, there is something here that should be investigated in much more depth in relation to the Mexican. In order to value himself highly, a person must feel at ease in various respects. He must have adequately taken advantage of the opportunities offered to him by life: opportunities to learn, to create, to work—in sum, to realize his being. A person must also feel more or less satisfied by what he does or has done in the past, in the sense that it is sufficiently well done. This could be a hobby, a profession, a sport, a craft, a work, or a duty. Well-done work is necessary in order for us to perceive ourselves with a certain satisfaction and with a certain appreciation of what we are worth. Now, if we can do this, we can value ourselves more or less highly; we can have confidence in ourselves. I believe that no one present here will doubt that we have a great need to feel confidence in ourselves. This can be said in other words. It seems obvious to say that every human being needs to feel capable and valuable, but it is less obvious that the need may be so intense that when it is insufficiently satisfied it can force us to dedicate the best of our energy and time—in short, the best of our lives—to satisfying it, whether by appropriate or by abnormal means. A person with sufficiently satisfied self-esteem will feel and enjoy the capacity to be independent and will have the feeling that, come what may, alone or accompanied, he can cope with what reality deals him. Such a person will have a high sense of human dignity and will love liberty. In fact, in order to appreciate and above all to need liberty intensely, it seems necessary that the prior needs of the hierarchy be more or less adequately met. We have already said that, if we are starving, liberty, love, sexuality, and even safety matter little; the problem is eating. But, if we have had sufficient opportunity to satisfy those other areas of need, we shall certainly have a powerful need for liberty.

Before abandoning this aspect of self-evaluation, I ought to mention something that seems very interesting to me: the fact that in the Spanish language we have no direct way to say "self-esteem" and that we have had to search for and almost coin the term *propia estima*, which sounds very awkward. It seems that in Spanish there is no expression that refers precisely to this human need.[5]

Could this be because we have not realized its importance? Could it have gone unnoticed because we have no way to refer to it? Because we find it difficult to satisfy in our environment, do we keep it to some extent unconscious? In any case, we shall see later that all this affects the attitudes of the Mexican, and most significantly those of the Mexican worker.

But we said that there are other considerations that are related to

[5] Different English-Spanish dictionaries translate *self-esteem* as *estimación de sí mismo, amor propio*, etc. In Eduardo Benot's *Diccionario de ideas afines*, in the section where the expression *estima de sí mismo* is cited, the following related ideas are found: *orgullo, altivez, arrogancia, amor propio, dignidad*, the Latin expression *meus sibi conscia recti, altanería, vanagloria, alteza de miras, soberbia, orgullo satánico, ínfulas*, etc. The great majority of these expressions obviously refer to the positive and negative extremes of the area concerned with self-esteem, with *orgullo satánico, altivez*, etc., at one end, and *alteza de miras, dignidad*, etc., at the other. *Dignidad* perhaps comes closest to what we mean when we speak of self-esteem, but even this expression is impregnated with other values and does not cover the whole extension of the area of self-esteem. It seems that in our language there is no way to express an adequate equilibrium of self-esteem. At present in the United States Dr. Anatol Rapoport ("General Semantics: Its Place in Science," *ETC.: A Review of General Semantics* 16, no. 1 [1958]: 80–97) and others are trying to investigate experimentally Whorf's affirmation that human beings can think only in their own language; that is, that they are incapable of thinking outside the expressions that belong to their own language. If this is true, we could affirm that the Spanish-Mexican group at least, because of various conditions of its history, sociology, etc., has never been able to think clearly through the problem of its self-esteem.

Rafael Porrúa has suggested to me the word *autoestima*, which seems to be the best translation to date.

self-esteem. They are the evaluations that others make of us. This refers to what we call, in common, everyday terms, a good reputation. In other words, it refers to the fact that we all need to be respected, admired, and praised, if not by all people, certainly by some; obviously we feel better the more others attribute to us ability, power, intelligence, likeability, beauty. On the other hand, the area of this need is sometimes defined in another form, and factors such as social position or the simple possession of money can be substituted for it; but, in any case, it has to do with being recognized, with attention being paid to what we say, to our ideas, to our ways of thinking and deciding. We all love to talk and be listened to—that is why I am here, talking away—and, in short, we all have a need to be appreciated and given some importance.

Now, the adequate satisfaction of the needs of self-esteem provokes a sensation of confidence in oneself, a sensation of personal value, of ability, of personal security, and even the satisfying sensation of feeling very well, "comfortable," as the preparatory-school youths of my generation used to say with great pleasure, besides feeling oneself needed in the world and useful to others.

If the satisfaction of these needs is blocked, people will generally demonstrate feelings of inferiority, of personal insecurity, at times even extremes of weakness and despair. Moreover, the same person, when he suffers from this condition of internal devaluation, can have all these feelings at once; we all have them from time to time, of course, but not chronically. If prolonged, the condition of which we have been speaking can provoke basic and chronic pessimism and, in some cases, even complete apathy. In other cases, manifestly abnormal tendencies can appear to compensate for the lack of valid self-esteem; in other words, a person will brag and bluster to a disturbing extent. What we do not have, we flaunt. Making a great effort to fool ourselves and fool others, we boast of possessing what we most lack.

There is another series of human needs even beyond those which we have just defined. Now you see how complicated we are in reality; that is why solutions to human problems, both individual and general, are slow in coming, for there are many factors to take into consideration. On one occasion I called this group of needs those of integral development of the personality. I believe, nevertheless, that the doctors Kurt Goldstein, Abraham H. Maslow, Carl R. Rogers, etc., have succeeded in better defining and elaborating these needs, which Goldstein has called *self-actualization*. What is involved here is the need for our abilities, our talents, our potentialities to have an opportunity to express themselves, to develop, to bear fruit, in short, to actualize themselves. All human beings contain a series of potentialities, many repressed, as Maslow maintains. This group of needs is not very strong, given its place in the hierarchy. But it can exhibit its power if the other needs are sufficiently satisfied. In our environment, because of the degree of frustration of other needs, these needs only rarely reach full expression, development, and actualization. At times, very rarely, to be sure, they appear with a certain force, but only substituting for other needs that do not succeed in expressing themselves; they rob the energy of those other needs but do not succeed in expressing their own nature, as they only reflect the mixture of needs that provoke them.

There are other groups of needs—the aesthetic, the cognitive, etc.— but those we have mentioned are the fundamental ones in relation to our present problem, that is, the problem of the motivations of the Mexican worker. But there also exist other needs that we ought to mention: learned needs. These needs that we learn to have are multiple and very diverse in nature. For example, no one is born with a desire to go to the movies; rather, one learns to go to the movies; a woman is not born with the specific desire to wear lipstick but rather learns to wear lipstick; and so on. But, of these learned needs, perhaps the most important ones for our talk here are the sociocultural needs, for the Mexican today faces a series of sociocultural factors so profound that we must take them into account. We see, for example, that it is almost definitively established that in general the Mexican male wants to be very *macho*, speaking in sociocultural terms. In fact, this need to be very masculine, in the specific Mexican sense, is indeed something quite characteristic and typical of the Mexican.[6]

---

[6] Or, perhaps, of the Latin American. See Essay 1 and E. D. Maldonado Sierra, Richard D. Trent, and R. Fernández Marina, "Three Basic Themes in Mexican

It is so extensive that the Mexican word *machismo* is used in some circles of North American psychologists to express the complex of attitudes that it embraces. Of course, the need to differentiate feminine and masculine roles exists in all cultures, but one must remember that this takes quite diverse forms.

In any case, we have at least clarified what motivation is. How shall we relate all this to the motivations of the Mexican worker? I really ought to caution you in advance: I am going to leap to a precipice of conclusion and express a series of hypotheses. I am going to make a small, hypothetical profile of the motivation of the Mexican worker. By *profile* I mean the enumeration of a series of needs that I believe to be important to a better understanding of the Mexican worker and the assigning to them of quantitative value. All this is tentative, but we must do it for a better understanding of this problem. To each hypothetical need. of the worker I am going to assign an intensity on a scale from one to ten. That is, minimum intensity will be assigned a value of one and maximum intensity will be assigned a value of ten. Now I am going to present my opinions as they come, so that we can discuss them afterwards, for, as I said earlier, you are in direct contact with the Mexican worker; I, on the other hand, am extrapolating to the Mexican worker what I have been able to investigate, observe, and read about the Mexican in general; therefore we must cooperate.

Hunger. Following the hierarchical order we have described, let us first consider physiological needs. I put hunger in first place. Why do I speak of hunger in relation to the Mexican worker? I believe that the Mexican worker is no stranger to hunger; I believe that in some cases he has opportunity in his existence to know what severe hunger is. In many other cases he has suffered partial hunger. We know, and various authors point out, that his nourishment is incomplete. Some people have gone so far as to declare that the fundamental characteristics of Mexican behavior are explained by the fact that the Mexican is not well nourished. S. Maynes Puente

———
and Puerto Rican Family Values," *Journal of Social Psychology* 48 (1958): 167–181.

holds this position, for example. Obviously we cannot agree with this "interpretive monism," since we have defended a criterion of multiplicity and relativity of needs. But we can easily understand why it has been said that the behavior of the Mexican is explained by his hunger. Maynes Puente recalls that Pito Pérez, when he said that "man is hunger [*el hombre es hambre*]," referred to strata of society with which we have only indirect contact.[7] In reality you executives have a closer contact. Considering all these factors, I give to hunger, as a need of the Mexican worker, a value of five, halfway between the minimum and maximum intensity.

Need for physical health. In relation to this need I had thought that the Mexican tends to be a hypochondriac, that he enjoys taking pills, going to a doctor or herbalist or charlatan in the street for medicines to improve his health. I am upheld in this belief by data obtained in a study carried out by the psychologist Victoria Zúñiga Oceguera.[8] When she applied the Minnesota Multiphasic Personality Inventory to a group of Mexicans, she found that, at least for this group, the scale of hypochondria showed a much higher level than it did for Americans. Nevertheless, another of my students, commenting on this, said, "I don't agree; I don't think the Mexican cares a bit about health; this is so true that he says, for example, 'Today I'm going on a spree and let tomorrow take care of itself'; he is so much this way that I have often seen him with a fever saying, 'Let's go on a binge, let tomorrow take care of itself, what do I care.' " This is related to the fact, which we shall see later, that the Mexican does not seem to have a sense of the need to preserve his own life. It is said that it is difficult to discipline Mexicans to observe safety measures in a factory. These must be facets of the famous Mexican attitude of "Why should I bother? God determines all." It would seem that in many ways Mexicans wish to demonstrate that they have little fear of life or death. The Villistas' famous roulette wheel of death shows

[7] S. Maynes Puente, "Los mexicanos analizados por sí mismos," *Excélsior* (Mexico City), August 3, 1958. (Pito Pérez is a character in the novel *La vida inútil de Pito Pérez* by José Rubén Romero.)

[8] Victoria Zúñiga Oceguera, "Estudios preliminares en México del inventario multifásico de la personalidad de Minnesota" (M.A. thesis, Universidad Nacional Autónoma de México, 1958).

us that, in fact, the question of living or dying has little importance for many Mexicans for reasons that are probably sociocultural in nature. But in this meeting of students there was another, a woman, and she said, "I, on the other hand, do agree that the Mexican is a hypochondriac who is too concerned for his health." The problem was becoming more complex. Then someone brought up the fact that Mexican women frequently say to Mexican males, "Take care of yourself, put on your scarf," or, when a child goes out, "Don't catch cold," and so on. Mexican women would seem to be great worriers about health, and the Mexican male would seem to be the careless one. Finally, neither I nor my students were able to come to a definitive agreement or conclusion, and I can only say that before the discussion I had given the need for physical health a value of seven, but after the discussion I lowered the value to five. There I leave it, very tentative like all the rest.

Sexual need. We have already indicated that sexual need is very highly intensified in the Mexican. It was also noted that this intensification is explained socioculturally; that is, for one reason or another, this among all the needs in our environment has been isolated and has been given an enormous importance that unfortunately can and, as we believe, does obscure other potentialities of the Mexican. In my opinion, sexuality is of great importance for the Mexican because it is a kind of compensation for other things that he lacks and that we will analyze farther on. Perhaps one of the best signs of the exaggeration of one need, in compensation for another, unfulfilled need or in compensation for its own failure to be satisfied, is boasting or bragging of that need's satisfaction. The more serious, the more chronic, and the more exaggerated this bragging, the greater is the lack of real satisfaction in other areas or the same area of need. Thus, when we assign sexuality an intensity of ten in our profile, we are emphasizing that the most intense need exists, but at the same time we explain that this total intensity is a combination of pure sexual need and necessity for vicarious satisfaction of other unsatisfied needs.

Fear of unemployment. We shall speak now of the fear of unemployment, another of the motivations that foreign authors have discussed in relation to workers. I must confess that it gave me a good bit of trouble to clarify this problem in relation to the Mexican worker. In reality I do not have sufficient direct knowledge of this situation. Indirectly one should infer that this fear must be quite intense because of the very issue of hunger as a motivation of the Mexican worker. But, on the other hand, many executives and employers are quite concerned by the high percentage of job changes observed among Mexican workers to date. How can we reconcile a high percentage of job terminations, seemingly voluntary for the most part, with an intense or fairly intense fear of unemployment? We know, in addition, that in the United States there is a high degree of fear of unemployment, so high that if we were making a profile of the American worker we would assign an intensity of nine or ten to this need. But we also know, from the classic studies of Paul Lazarsfeld and P. Eisenberg,[9] that this high degree of fear does not result from confronting a situation in which it is not possible to satisfy the basic physiological needs; on the contrary, everything seems to indicate that this intense fear of unemployment can be explained fundamentally as fear of losing self-esteem. This most interesting fact will acquire even greater significance a little later in this study. But the data just reported still do not seem to help resolve the apparent contradiction of a worker who has an intensity of five for the hunger need, but who apparently lacks fear of unemployment, given his habit of voluntarily leaving his job. Only by turning our eyes to a social factor, the Mexican family, can we find an explanation for the apparently unexplainable. The Mexican family is traditionally united and protective. There will almost always be a roof and a meal, and sometimes even an affectionate welcome, for the son, the brother, and even for the more distant relative who has lost his job. This is the classic "Don't worry, son; we'll make out all right; while I'm alive you'll lack for nothing." Thus, having to assign a specific intensity to fear of unemployment, and considering that the traditional Mexican socioculture has also been changing, aside from other aspects, we allow ourselves to assign to this need an intensity of five in our profile.

[9] Paul Lazarsfeld, "An Unemployed Village," *Character and Personality* 1 (1932): 147–151; P. Eisenberg and Paul Lazarsfeld, "The Psychological Effects of Unemployment," *Psychological Bulletin* 35 (1938): 358–390.

Economic motivation. Money is another very interesting factor for the Mexican. It is really a symbol and also a compensation for many other things; because of this, as much for its real value as for its symbolic value, I have assigned it an intensity of ten in our profile. The Mexican laborer values money highly, not in itself, but rather because he sees in it the solution to all his problems. To clarify for the Mexican laborer what money can do and what it cannot do might help to diminish his present unrealistic impression of its value. He is right in thinking that in general money eliminates hunger and fosters health, but he errs when he believes that it can satisfy his sexual need, even as he defines it, and much less in the aspects that his definition overlooks.

It would be very difficult for him to understand, and he would find it incredible, that for the most part the complete and satisfactory expression of sexuality cannot be achieved except when a sizable group of other needs, among them those of self-esteem, has been sufficiently satisfied. In any case, through the presence of some real factors and other false ones, money has high value for the Mexican, and the worker will be motivated by money; that is to say, if he is given more money he will do more. On the other hand, as Fritz J. Roethlisberger, William J. Dickson, and James A. Brown tell us[10]— and you yourselves will have had similar experiences—the motivation resulting from a salary increase improves the workers' efficiency only temporarily. To end this part of the discussion, let us note an interesting fact. In the poll I mentioned earlier, the following question was included: "Do you believe that a gift of five million pesos would solve *all your problems?*" Despite the absoluteness of this statement, 40 percent of the males above eighteen in Mexico City replied "yes."

Need for personal safety. We have indicated that, given what we might call the Mexican's *torero* complex, he does not seem to have a great need for personal safety in his work or outside it. I do not believe, therefore, that he cares very much whether or not his employers concern themselves with personal-safety measures at work. Given

[10] Fritz J. Roethlisberger and William J. Dickson, *Management and the Worker;* James A. Brown, *Social Psychology of Industry.*

the attitude of the Mexican, it is even rather difficult to make him accept and carry out consistently the safety measures adopted in a specific factory. To personal safety at work, *as motivation in the Mexican worker*, I give an intensity of only two in the profile.

Love and tenderness. We said that in general the Mexican seems not to need love and tenderness; even more, I believe that he does not realize that these factors can be the objects of an intense and open need among some human beings. We do not mean to say that the Mexican repudiates love and tenderness but rather, if I may express it this way, that he sits down at the table of love not with hunger but with appetite. In a good number of cases, the Mexican mother suffocates her infants with her tenderness; it is not uncommon to hear "Enough, enough, leave me alone," when affection, love, or tenderness is expressed to a Mexican. In any case, it is well to remember that this estimable affection and tenderness of the Mexican mother has in some cases, as we know, a special diagnosis and prognosis; and it is not uncommon that by exaggerating these tendencies she may provoke pathological dependencies in her children, as some studies have seemed to prove. In consequence I give these factors the value of one as a need of the Mexican worker.

Need for self-esteem. We have arrived at the most painful point of this lecture: not only because the Mexican's self-esteem is as low as can be, but also because we find ourselves before a situation so chronic, profound, and hopeless that in many ways external evidence seems to belie the fact that the self-esteem of the Mexican in general, and in particular of the Mexican worker, is at such a low point. By this, in preliminary and somewhat imprecise form, we mean that in the Mexican the need for self-esteem is so tremendously intense that he could even tend to deny its existence. To clarify further, let us say that it is possible that it hurts him so not to have adequate self-esteem that he feels forced to deny completely the existence of this need.

In this sense, the behavior of the Mexican in general is truly fascinating; it seems that he cannot find a way, sometimes for real reasons and other times for fictional reasons, to feel sufficiently sure of himself. It seems that it is totally impossible for him to value himself highly in relation to others and in relation to himself; it is as if he finds that in the midst of all this it is much easier to be a *bocón*, or "big mouth," bragging and boasting, than to make a serious and stable effort to find those multiple areas in which he does in fact have value, and in which he may constructively demonstrate his worth.

Also, due to this clear tendency toward boasting and the Mexican's exaggeration of his virile ability, of his *machismo*, it has been possible for anyone who has simply heard of the mode and functioning of the inferiority complex to diagnose the Mexican as the typical sufferer of this problem. Because of this it would seem that the doctrines of Alfred Adler were devised specifically to explain the personality of the Mexican. Dr. Samuel Ramos saw it thus, with profound clarity.[11] Dr. Ramos was the first to realize that it was not the Freudian system but the Adlerian that was appropriate to explain the idiosyncrasies of our nation; he was also the first to apply toward the understanding of the Mexican personality the concepts of dynamic psychology; nevertheless, he was unable, given his own formation and ability, to restrict himself to utilizing in original, limited form the concepts of the psychologist Adler. Thus, anticipating the whole later movement called anthropologic-cultural by the modern schools of psychoanalysis, he tells us with great precision and simplicity: "Adler states that the sense of inferiority appears in the boy when he becomes aware of the insignificance of his strength, compared to that of his parents. When Mexico was born, it found itself in the civilized world in the same relation as the child before his elders. It appeared in history when a mature civilization held sway, a civilization that only half understood an infantile spirit. From this disadvantageous situation was born the sense of inferiority that was ingrained by the Conquista, by *mestizaje* or crossbreeding, and even by the disproportionate magnitude of nature."[12] It is evident not only that Dr. Ramos was aware of the sense of inferiority of the Mexican, which is another way of saying the reaction to the realization of a low self-esteem, but also that he identified and added to the Adlerian dynamic explanation a series of historical and sociocultural factors that caused

[11] Samuel Ramos, *El perfil del hombre y la cultura en México*.
[12] Ibid.

the Mexican to develop a feeling of "less worth," as he calls it. This
expression of personal *menorvalía*[13] represents another effort, this
one made by Dr. Ramos, to express in Mexico the need for self-
esteem. When Ramos speaks in later pages about the way in which
this sense of inferiority affects people of different social classes, he
makes a series of extraordinary statements about the way in which
it is expressed and felt in each one of the categories. Anyone who
reads these statements by Ramos with care will notice almost an
exact correspondence with the symptoms we have described as results of the lack of satisfaction of the need for self-esteem.

Again, even though I am completely in agreement with Ramos
that a series of historical and sociocultural factors have influenced
this *menorvalía*, this lack of satisfaction of the need for self-esteem,
I also ought to add that of greater importance in the final result are
present-day sociocultural forces and, above all, the values that determine various characteristics of the Mexican family. Thus, socioculturally, an abuse of the concept of authority has, from time to
time, permitted the dignity and self-esteem of individuals to be
trampled on. The bossism against which we are fighting with more
determination now is still far from disappearing. In the Mexican
family it is the father who abuses authority.[14] We know that the
father, although affectionate in some ways, is first and foremost a
disciplinarian. And, although we may believe that a little authority
is always necessary in the development of children, its abuse is certainly detrimental. In addition—and this could be the fundamental
issue—the authority exercised by the father is irrational or, to put
it another way, is frequently unjust. The father beats the child for
the same thing that he earlier rewarded or approved. Unfortunately,
reward or punishment follows not from the behavior of the child
and from its consequences, but from the father's mood. The result
in all cases is the same. From early childhood the human being needs
to form the sense that he is worth something. His need for self-esteem

[13] The word *menorvalía* is not found in the *Diccionario de la Real Academia
Española* or in the *Pequeño Larousse Ilustrado*. In the absence of other evidence,
I conclude that Dr. Ramos coined the word.
[14] See Essay 9.

is already present. He frequently needs the satisfaction of actions well carried out. But, if even during infancy there is no logical way to construct self-esteem on real bases, we can easily conclude that the Mexican begins the history of his life with his self-esteem already destroyed. Even more, given the prevalent economic conditions, historical as well as present, there has been little opportunity for the Mexican to develop his self-esteem, since the most intense physiological needs, like hunger, whether of the individual or of his family, have often been active.

I have the impression—and this is the central point of my thesis about motivation—that the Mexican worker is hungry, deeply hungry to develop his self-esteem, but that, having arrived at a profound state of humiliation in relation to this need, he can react with excessive sensitivity. To clarify, apart from the lively resistance that a braggart will put up when told there is nothing to brag about, there can be another type of reaction caused by low self-esteem. This type of reaction, which is somewhat more subtle and may be found in persons of greater mental development, covers the absence of self-esteem with a thick layer of oversensitivity. We have the case of those people who react to praise with displeasure. I can easily think of an example; one tells a person, "Congratulations for having obtained these results or for having done this work so well." And the person answers, "Don't make fun of me," or "Don't say that; I don't like to have people tell me that things are well done," and so on. That is, in certain cases it is pride that takes on the appearance of a fundamental or intense lack of self-esteem. But, in short, if all this that we have been theorizing about and trying to demonstrate as certain were in fact certain, we would really have established a highly important aspect of the motivation of the Mexican worker. Then industrial psychology could attempt, little by little, to investigate and find solutions for this sensitive problem of Mexican self-esteem, because I profoundly believe that through this gradual development, and not through economically unrealistic salary raises, the Mexican can become a better worker; that is, he can come to feel essentially and basically that he is worth something, that his work is important, that it is valuable for the development of other things, that what he does contributes to the development and progress of his country, of his family, and of human beings in general.

I have the impression too that we are in the appropriate historical moment, because in various respects the Mexican has begun to come out from his feeling of insecurity and is beginning, in a hesitant way, to realize that he does have real value, with which he can undertake the development of a deserved pride in himself and in belonging to the Mexican sociocultural group. In so far as he may do all this instead of bragging about his multiple triumphs in seduction, to that same extent he will have achieved the satisfaction of his need for self-esteem, and as a result he will be able to continue growing toward increasingly higher and wider horizons. But, in so far as he continues to brag of his ability to perform the sexual act a thousand times in a row, he will have only the momentary exhilaration derived from this resounding but empty shout, and he will fall immediately afterward into the profound abyss of his useless reality, unless he shouts again. Only by keeping up this shout, bragging, boasting, and showing off, can he feel himself temporarily invested with a self-esteem based totally on these aspects that seem to him, as to a certain point they are, invested with drama. In addition, the selection of sexuality and virile aggressiveness to brag about has not been made by chance. It implies a reiteration of something that is without exaggeration an aspect of valid and adequate raising of self-esteem: fulfilling the masculine role with dignity and pride.

The unsatisfied need for self-esteem also explains to us why the Mexican needs to talk incessantly with his friends and why he really needs so many friends, despite the fact that his need to affiliate should already be perfectly satisfied. The fact is that in friendship and in its exaggerated development can be found the easiest and most felicitous means of maintaining self-esteem. The intense power of this need can be seen in sexual bragging, as well as in the incessant search for close friends and for the understanding and completely accepting attitude of the "best friend." With friends one can brag without the criticism that demands evidence. Friends, as much in need of that self-esteem given by bragging as the speaker, are the most cooperative audience that could be hoped for, and they in turn will brag in the same way. Sometimes, unexpectedly, in the midst of its groping efforts, this bragging finally finds a more or less happy and more or less healthy avenue of expression. There are times when the braggart boasts in such an obvious, ridiculous, or comical manner that he provokes the laughter of his audience; then, suddenly, as often happens in the course of these incredible but magnificent changes that occur in psychological life, what was an inadequate compensation is transformed into a suitable form to develop self-esteem, through a healthy, profound, active, and original sense of humor. On occasions the braggart is transformed into a constructive being, into a being who can brag while laughing at himself. These Mexicans who are able to laugh at themselves and enjoy it have liberated themselves from the abnormal compensatory need and have found a positive aspect, a valid means of developing self-esteem through a healthy sense of humor. Of course, those who are able to discover the comic aspect of bragging frequently are those persons who in other aspects of life have succeeded in obtaining a certain degree of valid self-esteem, that is, the feeling of satisfaction of a job well done, of an opportunity taken advantage of, etc.

But in any case, this constant search for friends, so intense and so characteristic of our socioculture, is partially explained by the need to find, as we said, in these smiling and accepting faces a garden in the midst of a desert of low self-esteem. But we do not wish to oversimplify and say that friendship in the Mexican is based exclusively on this need, because in this accepting environment the Mexican often develops several of his high potentials with greater ease. The greatest creative efforts of our culture are produced in contact with friends. It is for this reason that I find incisively certain, and incisively perceptive, an assertion made by Angel de Campo (in Micrós) and cited by Maynes Puente in his interesting scrutiny of the Mexican's preoccupations. Angel de Campo, a literary figure and journalist of the last century, said in reference to Mexicans: "Each of us has a novel in his head; but inspiration escapes through our mouths, and we should look for the works of our genius not in pamphlets, in bookstores or in libraries, but in bars, cafés, corridors, newspaper premises, offices [I would add: factories], intimate visits, and after-dinner discussions."[15]

With the temporary feeling of high esteem that it provokes in those who take part, the environment of friendship is sufficiently fertile to bring to the surface the lost vocations, the obscured poten-tials, and the deep and creative aspects of the Mexican's personality. But this area has been sufficiently dealt with for the purposes of this study. Before turning to the next need of the Mexican worker, let us indicate that, given the circumstances to which we have been refer-ring, we firmly believe that the Mexican's need for self-esteem de-mands the highest rating possible in our profile, a value of ten. We note once more that this need, given the complexity of its formation and deformation in the Mexican, is partially conscious, partially semi-conscious, and to some degree unconscious.

Need for integral development or self-actualization. Given the varying degrees of satisfaction of many of the Mexican's physiolog-ical and psychological needs, we find that the need to create, to de-velop individual potential, frequently fails to achieve motivating force. At the same time, even when other needs are unfulfilled, the creative need in certain cases can be intense enough to be developed, not so much through its own force, however, as in compensation for many other needs. We do not know to what extent (and we do not believe ourselves capable of penetrating deeply into this problem at present) the artistic production of the "three masters" of Mexican painting can be interpreted this way; their painting is aesthetically valuable, but in its intensity and breadth and in its tremendous need to cover in great extension the problems, conflicts, and needs of the Mexican people, at the same time that it deals with infamous and historical abuse, first during the Conquest and later by multiple and varied interests, their painting may represent a psychological compensation for the artists. We do not know to what point their creation is impelled by artistic need and to what point and with what

[15] Maynes Puente, "Los mexicanos analizados por sí mismos."

force it is impelled by the unsatisfied needs of the artists, who, as historical representatives of the general condition of the Mexican, project themselves on those wide surfaces, leaving an unmistakable sign of many things that we have been saying. Therefore we will assign this need for integral development an intermediate value of five, since in many forms and whenever he has had the opportunity the Mexican has expressed his creativity; in effect, each one of us carries within himself his romantic and fanciful novel.

Need to improve the physical environment of the factory. My opinion is that improvements in the physical environment of the factory do not matter to the Mexican worker. Nevertheless—and perhaps this could be explored, or perhaps you yourselves can explain it to me afterwards through your own knowledge of these things—I believe that the Mexican worker might very well recognize improvements in the physical environment, not so much for what they signify in terms of health or efficiency, but as a form of recognition of his worth; that is, in one way or another he can interpret such improvements as affirmations that the employers have him in mind, that they attribute to him a certain importance, that they pay him a certain amount of attention. If the Mexican worker perceives such improvements in this way, they can act as a tool not only to improve his self-esteem, but also, vicariously, to improve his efficiency in work. In any case, we assign an intensity of only one to the specific need of the Mexican worker for improvements in the physical environment of the factory.

Technical improvement of the worker. I assign here an intensity of six in our profile, despite the fact that, given his general circumstances, the Mexican ought to have a need of ten for such technical improvement. Such an improvement would permit him to obtain many things that he believes he desires and others that he really does desire. But we are still touching on an aspect of the need for self-esteem. In effect, when the Mexican brags, he is not simply better, but perfect; therefore, if it is pointed out to him how to improve or how he ought to do things, he easily feels insulted. On the other hand, I am sure that he feels the need to improve, recognizing that he ought to improve his technical knowledge. One of the questions of the survey that we have cited so often asked: "Does it annoy you to be told how to do things?"[16] Sixty-three percent of Mexican males over eighteen years old in Mexico City answered "yes." We see that in fact there does exist here a definite area of sensitivity in the Mexican. Once more we insist that this is the fundamental problem that Mexico's psychologists, sociologists, etc., ought to try to solve before any other. Technical improvement of the worker will meet with resistance, a resistance provoked by his oversensitivity, which can be appropriately and completely overcome only through what we might call industrial psychotherapy.

Need to belong. James A. Brown, in *Social Psychology of Industry,* and Erich Fromm in his *Psicoanálisis de la sociedad contemporánea* (the former more than the latter) say that the factory is fundamentally a place of socializing.[17] They wish to convince us that one of the fundamental motives of the workman in his job is to participate as a member, to belong as an individual to the social group of the factory. As we have amply seen, the Mexican socializes everywhere and up to a certain point is fully satisfied in his sociability. The Mexican family as a closed group with intense bonds has satisfied, at times with exaggeration, this need to belong to a group. In consequence we do not believe that the Mexican will find much satisfaction in the factory, which cannot even be compared with the external environment, let us say, of family and ceremonial fiestas. We do not believe that he goes to the factory in search of the satisfaction of these needs. I believe that both Fromm and Brown are speaking of needs that are indeed powerful in other cultures. We could accept the idea that members of the American culture, possibly for lack of intense family bonds, need to search for human affection, friendship, or interpersonal relationships in the factory. The need for love is not so important for the Mexican, because it is sufficiently satisfied, and it is our opinion that he does not need to search for social life in the factory;

---

[16] See Essay 4.

[17] Brown, *Social Psychology of Industry*; Erich Fromm, *Psicoanálisis de la sociedad contemporánea.*

we will also say that, in general, solitude is no misfortune for the Mexican. If we are to believe Octavio Paz,[18] we must say that solitude is his "cup of tea." Fromm, among some interesting suggestions about ways to improve the situation of the workers, praises the communitarian movement in Europe and work communes.[19] My impression is that most Mexican workers would feel tremendously frightened if they had to belong to and participate in one of those closed communities of workers that Fromm describes. I believe that many of his points definitely do not apply to the Mexican, and I even feel that the solution to the various problems that Fromm points out does not lie in the factories, but rather that these problems ought to be resolved much earlier, in a kind of socialization much more essential for the human being. Those needs should be resolved in the bosom of the family. Therefore, I assign an intensity of one in the profile to the need for socializing within the factory.

Need for entertainment. To conclude, let us speak of this need in the Mexican. Judging from the lines to get into movies, from the many sports that attract the public in great numbers, from the prevalence of holidays and of ceremonial celebrations, from the celebration of saints' days as well as of birthdays, it seems that the Mexican has a great need for entertainment. To be entertained and distracted is very important for the Mexican worker. What does he want to be distracted from? On one hand, I believe that he wants to be distracted from himself in what relates to his self-esteem; on the other I believe that he wants to forget many factors in the external reality in which he lives. But I do not believe that these points exclusively explain this need for entertainment; I believe that in entertainment the Mexican achieves a feeling of well-being and feels himself capable of creating, although it may all be only dreaming and fantasizing. From the shows in which the Mexican is permitted open expression one forms the impression that he is going to take part in the performance in some way, to participate in it. The ingenious shouts, the applause, the enthusiasm, and the laughter indicate that he creates

---

[18] Octavio Paz, *El laberinto de la soledad.*
[19] Fromm, *Psicoanálisis de la sociedad contemporánea.*

while he observes. At the movies, where open participation is reduced, the Mexican frequently lives other lives by identifying himself with certain characters in the film. In this area we also find the combination of various unsatisfied needs of the Mexican worker. And, to end so long a disquisition, we assign a value of ten in our profile to the need for entertainment.

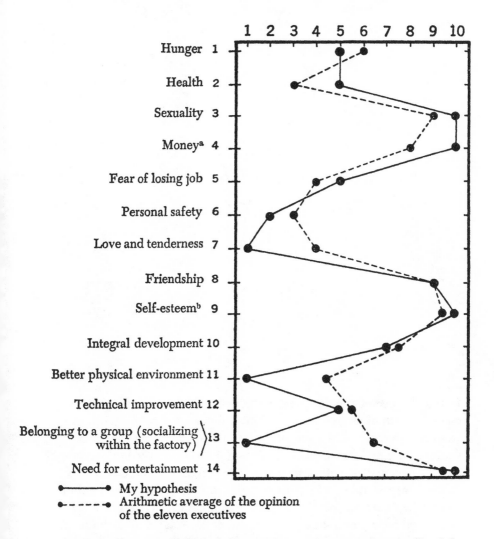

Figure 3–1
Hypothetical Profile of the Motivation of the Mexican Worker

NOTE. After my talk I asked the executives present to make a profile of the Mexican worker using the needs discussed, independently and based on their own experience. Eleven executives participated in the round table. The arithmetic average of their evaluations was as follows: hunger, 5.8; health, 3.1; sexuality, 9.2; money, 7.5; fear of losing job, 3.6; personal safety, 2.6; love and tenderness, 3.5; friendship, 9.3; self-esteem, 9.5; integral development, 7.3; better physical environment, 4.4; technical improvement, 5.5; belonging to a social group in the factory, 7.1; entertainment, 9.5.

a "Money" represents symbolically, but with partial error, the solution of all needs.

b To maintain self-esteem, in my opinion, is the most powerful need of the Mexican worker. Due to its intensity, it can be sought not only directly but also under various masks: sexuality, money, etc.

4. The Mental, Personal, and Social Health of the Mexican of Mexico City

Problem

In the absence of standardized methods for determining the level of mental health of large groups, and even though our primary purpose was to investigate the psychology of the Mexican, we decided to venture, first, to form a concept of mental health that would include various personal as well as social aspects and that would be founded as much as possible on facts of recognized value within the field of mental hygiene; second, to determine a practical and more or less valid method of compiling data necessary for establishing the level of mental disorder in Mexico City; at the same time we wished to dig into some factors that seem to affect the incidence of mental illness or disorder in our environment.

We should make clear from the start that the present work is only a superficial beginning of theory and method; it is being published only so that it may be criticized, in hopes that these criticisms may

NOTE. This study was published under the title "Teoría y resultados preliminares de un ensayo de determinación del grado de salud mental, personal y social del mexicano de la ciudad," *Psiquis* 2, nos. 1–2 (1952): 31–56. It has been translated by Cecile C. Wiseman.

serve to improve both the theory and the method; then we will undertake more extensive investigations.

After various discussions, and under the influence of concepts derived from modern psychological science and other concepts, such as those produced by scientific semanticists,[1] we concluded that for the purposes of this work the level of mental health of groups and individuals could be measured according to two fundamental concepts called *rigidity* and *plasticity*.

Each of the concepts involves a cluster of factors, some of which we have tried to identify and later define in operational form, that is, in the form of conduct or attitudes that are observable or measurable in one way or another. It has been proposed that the concepts of plasticity and rigidity should refer to the extremes of the same scale with an infinite number of points in between. The concept of percentages seem to lend itself quite well to the description of such a scale between extremes. Plasticity, from our point of view, refers to a cluster of abilities whose level of development in the individual or group seems to be positively correlated with the level of mental health.[2] Plasticity means: (*a*) the level of ability of an individual or a group to *see, understand,* and *accept* the points of view of other individuals or groups (related concept: tolerance); (*b*) the level of objectivity or impartiality with which individuals or group members see their own point of view or their needs or their actions (related concepts: objectification of the ego and avoidance of immoderate use of defense mechanisms); (*c*) the level of ability to see, understand, and accept projects to be realized in the future that eventually redound to the material and spiritual benefit of the individual and of society (related concepts: ability to defer the satisfaction of impulses and needs—delay of reward; the Freudian reality principle); (*d*) the level of mental health measured by the number of incapacitating or distressing symptoms; (*e*) the level of inhibition of behavior (and of situations of conflict and frustration) provoked by sociocultural ideals and norms (related concept: the dynamic ego-superego); (*f*) the level of ignorance and animism (related concept: the "Korzyb-

[1] See Appendix 1.
[2] The validity of these concepts is discussed in Appendix 1.

skian identification"). Naturally, rigidity or level of rigidity means precisely the opposite.

Once we had clarified the form in which some concepts of mental hygiene could be converted into quasi-operational concepts, it was necessary to explain the method which could yield answers more or less valid in reference to the mental hygiene of large groups, like the group of Mexican inhabitants of Mexico City. Despite its various defects,[3] for the first tentative investigation, to which we refer in this study, we chose the method of survey by questionnaire. We were brought to this decision by an idea that later was confirmed to a certain extent: that Mexicans, even the city dwellers, are not used to personality studies and distrust them; it seemed to us that the poll, allowing them to remain anonymous and unknown to the investigator, would permit them greater liberty of expression than other methods of investigating large groups, such as the interview in depth of a representative sample.

Having decided on the poll with questionnaires, we confronted all the problems of the validity and reliability of polls.

One problem was the selection of questions that could measure the categories of rigidity-plasticity to which we have referred. The groups of questions were made up in accordance with the purpose of this preliminary poll, with a limited number of questions in each category.[4] We sought to obtain an idea of the class of questions that could give more or less appropriate results.

Our plan for the future is to design questionnaires that will individually investigate in depth each category within the concepts of plasticity and rigidity. Thus, instead of a reduced number, a greater number of questions can be included in each category, and this will provide greater possibilities for studying reliability and validity.

It was thought that categories 1 and 2 could be taken as one category that would measure the level of objectivity toward others and

---

[3] See Quinn McNemar, "Opinion Attitude Methodology," *Psychological Bulletin* 43, no. 4 (1946); Herbert S. Conrad, "The Validity of Personality Inventories in Military Practice," *Psychological Bulletin* 45, no. 5 (1948).

[4] The questions in each category can be examined in Tables 4-1–4-5.

toward oneself; although this supposition may be erroneous, it was accepted.

The following questions were typical of this category. Question 1: Does it annoy you to be told how to do things? Question 2: Do you always try to get your own way? An affirmative answer to these questions was naturally considered as an indication of rigidity in categories 1 and 2; a negative answer, as an indication of plasticity.

The following questions are typical of category 3, the ability to see projects to be realized in the future that redound to the benefit of the individual and the group. Question 1: Do you believe that Mexico should work out its own future without regard to other nations? Question 2: Would you be willing to give 1 percent of your annual income to increase the number of schools? Negative answers to the first question and positive answers to the second question were taken as signs of plasticity in this area.

The following questions are typical of category 4. Question 4: Are you a nervous person? Question 6: Do you often feel very depressed? An affirmative answer to these questions will indicate rigidity in category 4 and, in this case, evidence of the incapacitating symptoms.

Questions typical of category 5 are the following. Question 2: Do you believe that woman's place is in the home? Question 4: Do you believe it is proper for women to go out alone with men? An affirmative answer to the first question and a negative answer to the second question demonstrate rigidity of sociocultural origin.

Finally, the following questions are typical of category 6. Question 2: Do you believe that black cats, broken mirrors, or certain numbers bring good or bad luck? Question 1: Do you believe that a gift of five million pesos would solve all your problems? Affirmative answers to these questions denote signs of rigidity in this area.

The reasons for assigning rigidity or plasticity to the answers are discussed in Appendix 1.

Once the groups of questions were chosen, other problems had to be confronted: the method of distributing the questionnaires and a way of achieving a representative sample of subjects in Mexico City.

Following one of the simplest methods of public-opinion studies,[5] we obtained the percentages of individuals over eighteen years old in different occupations from Mexico City's 1940 population census, corrected for June 30, 1948.[6]

Table 4-6 shows the distribution of the population according to occupation. This information enabled us to apply the method of "weighted representative sampling."[7]

To use this method, we had to distribute the questionnaires proportionately in areas where independent evidence indicated that the greatest number of individuals belonging to the desired occupational categories would be found.

Since this information could not be obtained from the Department of Statistics, various institutions and individuals were consulted,[8] and finally a map was drawn, indicating areas of the city (colonias) that, according to the evidence obtained, should contain a preponderance of persons of the desired classifications.

The next step was to obtain the cooperation of a group of individuals with some knowledge of the technique employed. A group of students was chosen, most of them majoring in psychology, and they were given three lectures concerning the method of distribution and collection of the questionnaires. The questionnaire was in the form shown in Appendix 2. This questionnaire contains some questions analyzed not in this study but in an earlier one.[9]

Results

Of the 516 questionnaires distributed according to the method described, we obtained cooperation in 294 cases. That is, only 57% of the people chosen cooperated. This fact perhaps may not seem so negative if it is borne in mind that in studies of public opinion with

[5] See George H. Gallup, A Guide to Public Opinion Polls.

[6] Secretaría de la Economía Nacional, Dirección General de Estadística, Sexto censo de la población, 1948.

[7] See Malcolm Cantril, Gauging Public Opinion.

[8] Lazlo Radvanyi, Instituto Científico de la Opinión Pública Mexicana (verbal communication).

[9] William Possidente, "A Psychological Study of Public Opinion in Mexico" (M.A. thesis, Mexico City College Library).

one or few questions Malcolm Cantril has obtained an approximate cooperation of 67% in large cities of the United States.[10] Cantril believes that the results are not greatly affected by this lack of cooperation; others, like Quinn McNemar, doubt that he is correct.[11] In any case, we ought to point out that our results are based on that group of the population with sufficient plasticity to participate in answering the questionnaire.

Table 4-7 shows the percentage of cooperation by areas. Owing to irregular cooperation in different areas, the hypothesis that certain areas contain a greater number of persons with a specific occupation could be neither proved nor disproved. Also, it seems that in our questionnaire people are classified, on various occasions, according to a classification different from that used in the census. Thus the group that cooperated correlates only in certain occupations with the percentages indicated in the census. In any case, given the diversity of regions of the city where questionnaires were distributed randomly (each third house of various streets in a *colonia*), we can assume that the poll is actually based on the use of clusters and random sampling from these clusters.

With the limits defined in the preceding lines, we may turn to the analysis and discussion of the results.

Tables 4-8 and 4-9 show the results of questions classified within categories 1 and 2 of plasticity and rigidity. The Mexican of Mexico City acts or thinks rigidly in these categories 34% (± 2.82%) of the time. That is, one of every three Mexicans of Mexico City responds rigidly. On the other hand, since the average of the "plastic" answers is 55% ± 2.82%, it should be noted that more than one of every two Mexicans responds plastically in this area. Since, as is explained in Appendix 1, rigid responses in this area are associated with conflict and frustration, and therefore with mental instability, one of every three Mexicans of Mexico City is highly predisposed toward poor mental health. As Table 4-9 shows, the results for this group of questions differ little for men and women, and statistics confirm that there

---

[10] Cantril, *Gauging Public Opinion.*
[11] McNemar, "Opinion Attitude Methodology."

is no significant difference between the sexes in these categories of rigidity-plasticity, as measured by the present scale.

Table 4-10 and 4-11 show the results in category 3. We disagree with this scale and believe that the questions in it were poorly chosen. The results indicate for the whole group a rigidity of 24% ± 2.45% and a plasticity of 65% ± 2.83%. If the scale were valid, this would indicate that approximately one of every four Mexicans thinks or makes decisions rigidly about plans whose fruits are projected into the distant future. It would also indicate that three of every four answer adequately, plastically, to these plans.

Tables 4-12 and 4-13 express the results of the scales that measure category 4. We believe that this is the most valid scale of those used. The results are extremely interesting. It will be recalled that here rigidity is measured by the percentage of incapacitating or distressing symptoms that psychiatry and psychology have traditionally considered as the best signs of abnormality or mental disturbance. The results indicate that among all the individuals in the poll there are 33% ± 2.64% rigidity and 62% ± 2.82% plasticity. This can be interpreted in the following way: on the average, 33% of the individuals who respond show in their answers a high degree of mental disorder or "neurosis"; on an average, one of every three Mexicans of Mexico City often becomes angry and feels depressed, takes offense easily, does not believe that life is worth living, suffers from bile, finds it difficult to concentrate, dislikes the work with which he earns his living, considers himself a nervous person, etc. Therefore it can perhaps be stated that one of every three Mexicans of Mexico City is maladjusted or neurotic.

But perhaps more interesting than this is the result derived from considering men and women of the city separately on this scale. We find that the average rigidity of the women is 44%, while that of the men is only 32%, and that feminine plasticity is 49%, as opposed to 62% in the males. The differences between these percentages are statistically significant at the level of 0.4% for rigidity and 0.9% for plasticity. The difference, therefore, is significant and indicates that maladjustment or neurosis is definitively greater in the Mexican woman than in the male. Of every two Mexican women of Mexico

City, one is maladjusted or neurotic, while this is true of only one of every three males. This is extremely interesting, because it clearly indicates that there have to be factors in the psycho-sociocultural environment of the city that lead to greater mental instability in the woman than in the man.

In any case, if we trust this scale, there is a high level of mental disease even among the men, and it is imperative that more detailed investigations be carried out to determine the factors that produce such extensive mental disorder.

Tables 4-14 and 4-15 indicate the total results of both sexes in category 5 of rigidity-plasticity. The results indicate that for the whole group, as well as for men and women considered separately, there is approximately 70% rigidity; that is, for the group of question-situations enumerated, 70% (± 2.64%) of the individuals are inhibited in their behavior by sociocultural norms. In Appendix I we will discuss the significance of this rigidity, which sustains ideals that apparently interfere with the individual's adaptation to a continually changing environment.

Finally, Tables 4-16 and 4-17 indicate a rigidity in ignorance and animism for the whole group of 32% (± 2.64%). It can be seen that there is little difference in this scale between men and women. The percentage of those answering "I don't know" is significantly (20%) higher among the women than among the men, perhaps indicating a sincere recognition of ignorance in regard to the questions.

Since this study is a simple attempt to measure mental health in large groups, through operational definitions of various concepts of mental health and through the method of the questionnaire, we will not spend much time discussing the results.[12] We only want to point out that the percentages of rigidity and plasticity of scales 1–2, 4, and 6 and their standard error seem to indicate, within the limitations of this study, that areas of thought and action are being measured that may show correlations among themselves, so that factors of scales 1–2 and 6 can well contribute much more directly than appears at first glance to the incapacitating symptoms shown in scale 4. It is interest-

[12] If we had carried out this study in 1960, instead of 1949, we would have used Chi square as a statistic instead of the ones used then.

ing that scale 5 should show such a high level of rigidity. This result could perhaps have been foreseen; the Mexican frequently defends the concepts of this scale as immutable: these sociocultural norms are probably among the most rigid of those most rigidly implanted in the national scene. Often Mexicans consider such values as primordial and almost natural or inherent characteristics of Mexican nationality. One often hears that what is Mexican should be preserved, and it is not rare for any attempt at change in these spheres to be considered as traitorous to the Mexican nation. Ramón López Velarde, a poet deeply Mexican in temperament, alerts Mexicans in his *Suave patria*: "They want to kill your spirit and your style" and exhorts, "Be always the same, faithful to your daily mirror."[13] From the point of view of mental hygiene, it would be well to discuss these points in more depth. Mexico has changed profoundly with the Mexican Revolution and with recent industrialization; it is probably ill-advised to maintain norms that no longer reflect the reality of present-day Mexico. Traditions, like old maps, may well fail to represent the many newly added territories; thus they inevitably contribute to frustration and conflict, and therefore to unhappiness or mental instability.

In Appendix 1 we will consider in more depth the implications of scale 5 of this questionnaire.

Conclusions

1. This study represents a preliminary effort to measure the mental health of large groups.

2. An attempt is made to determine areas of what is called mental health and to define operationally some factors that play a part in the mental health of individuals and groups.

3. The method chosen is that of a poll by a questionnaire containing scales that measure, by means of percentages of adequate and inadequate responses, the level of mental health of individuals and the group.

4. An effort is made to distribute the questionnaires to a represent-

[13] Ramón López Velarde, *Poesías completas*, 2d ed., pp. 264–270.

ative sample in proportion to occupations, in accordance with the 1940 census.

5. Only 57% of the public cooperates, and the distribution by occupations does not correlate with the distribution found in the census. Nevertheless, the method is considered to be that of the randomly chosen representative sample. Only individuals eighteen years old or over participate.

6. Scales 1–2 and 6 show a rigidity of approximately 33% in the answers.

7. Scale 4, considered more valid, shows that, of every three Mexicans of Mexico City, one is maladjusted or neurotic. Women are significantly more neurotic than men. Of every two women of the city, one is maladjusted or neurotic, according to the scale. This is true of only one man of every three.

8. Scale 5 shows a rigidity of 70%. This scale measures sociocultural norms deeply rooted in Mexico. At present there seems to be little desire to change them. It is indicated that they can well be a source of conflict for the Mexican.

It is indicated that the rigidity measured by scales 1–2 and 6, and perhaps by 5, has some relation to the evident state of mental instability of the Mexican of Mexico City.

9. Scale 3 shows a rigidity of 24%. There are indications that it does not satisfy the definition of the area that it attempts to measure.

Table 4-1

Tentative Questions in Categories 1 and 2 (Tolerance
and Objectification of the Ego)

	Yes	No
1. Does it annoy you to be told how to do things?		X
2. Do you always try to get your own way?		X
3. If someone should show you that your way of life is not good, would you change?	X	
4. Do you think that many of your desires are contrary to your moral and religious ideas?	X	
5. If you are a man, do you feel that you are more of a man than others?		X
6. Do you believe that it is natural for married men to have mistresses?		X
7. Do you believe that men are more intelligent than women?		X
8. Do you believe that a dictatorship would be beneficial for Mexico?		X
9. If you believe in certain ideals, would you abandon them for the common good?	X	
10. Do you believe that the stricter the parents are, the better the children turn out?		X

NOTE. When the questions are answered as shown, plasticity in areas 1 and 2 is indicated.

Table 4-2

Tentative Questions in Category 3 (Ability to See Projects
of Delayed Realization, "Reality Principle")

	Yes	No
1. Do you believe that Mexico should work out its own future without regard to other nations?		X
2. Would you be willing to give 1 percent of your annual income to increase the number of schools?	X	
3. If you believe in certain ideals, would you abandon them for the common good?	X	
4. Do you believe that honest politicians are stupid?		X

	Yes	No
5. Do you believe that someone who accepts a bribe is shrewd?		X
6. Do you believe that maids should work only eight hours a day?	X	

NOTE. When the questions are answered as shown, plasticity in area 3 is indicated.

Table 4-3

Tentative Questions in Category 4 (Incapacitating or Distressing Mental Symptoms)

	Yes	No
1. Are you happier alone than in company?		X
2. Do you get angry frequently?		X
3. Do you think life is worth living?	X	
4. Are you a nervous person?		X
5. Do you take offense easily?		X
6. Do you often feel very depressed?		X
7. *a.* Do you like the type of work with which you earn your living?	X	
b. If you are a housewife, do you like housework?	X	
8. Do you get along better with friends than with members of your family?		X
9. Do you believe in trusting people?	X	
10. Do you find it difficult to concentrate on what you read or study?		X
11. Do you frequently suffer from bile?		X

NOTE. When the questions are answered as shown, plasticity in area 4 is indicated.

Table 4-4

Tentative Questions in Category 5 (Inhibition of Behavior Provoked by Sociocultural Norms)

	Yes	No
1. Is your mother for you the dearest person in existence?		X
2. Do you believe that woman's place is in the home?		X

	Yes	No
3. Do you believe that men should "wear the pants in the family"?		X
4. Do you believe it is proper for women to go out alone with men?	X	
5. Do you believe that the stricter the parents are, the better the children turn out?		X
6. Do you believe that maids should organize in unions to improve their condition?	X	

NOTE. When the questions are answered as shown, plasticity in area 5 is indicated.

Table 4-5

Tentative Questions in Category 6 (Ignorance and Animism)

	Yes	No
1. Do you believe that a gift of five million pesos would solve all your problems?		X
2. Do you believe that black cats, broken mirrors, or certain numbers bring good or bad luck?		X
3. Do you believe that men are more intelligent than women?		X
4. Do you think that a dictatorship would be beneficial for Mexico?		X
5. If you believe in certain ideals, would you abandon them for the common good?	X	
6. Do you believe that science can solve most human problems?	X	
7. Do you believe that the stricter the parents are, the better the children turn out?		X

NOTE. When the questions are answered as shown, plasticity in area 6 is indicated.

Table 4-6
Adult Population of Mexico City in July, 1948,
Classified by Occupation

Classification	Total	(%)
1. Directors, managers	1,848	0.2
2. Private employees	70,690	6.7
3. Laborers	186,332	17.7
4. Individuals who help their families	2,503	0.2
5. Small-scale merchants	136,089	12.9
6. Servants	88,180	8.4
7. Public employees	56,555	5.4
8. Independent professionals	17,479	1.7
9. Unpaid domestic workers: housewives, etc.	447,719	42.4
10. Students	46,846	4.4
Total	1,054,241	100.0

NOTE. Both men and women are included. This is the population of individuals eighteen years old or over.

Table 4-7
Percentage of Cooperation by Areas in Order of
Diminishing Percentage

Area	Questionnaires Distributed	Questionnaires Returned	Cooperation (%)
Students (UNAM)	15	15	100
San Angel Inn	8	6	75
Peralvillo	62	45	73
Balbuena	39	27	69
Guerrero	29	20	69
Del Valle	53	35	66
Centro	43	27	63
Moderna	87	47	54
Santa María	26	14	54
San Rafael	68	29	43
Polanco	22	8	36
Cuauhtémoc	64	21	33
Totals	516	294	57

Table 4-8
Answers to Questions in Categories 1 and 2 (Tolerance,
Objectification of the Ego)

	Total Group		
	Rigidity (%)	Plasticity (%)	Don't Know (%)
1. Does it annoy you to be told how to do things?	34	63	3
2. Do you always try to get your own way?	44	53	3
3. If someone should show you that your way of life is not good, would you change?	24	64	12
4. Do you think that many of your desires are contrary to your moral and religious ideas?	64	29	7
5. If you are a man, do you feel that you are more of a man than others?	23	67	10
6. Do you believe that it is natural for married men to have mistresses?	20	70	10
7. Do you believe that men are more intelligent than women?	36	50	14
8. Do you believe that a dictatorship would be beneficial for Mexico?	28	52	20
9. If you believe in certain ideals, would you abandon them for the common good?	30	48	22
10. Do you believe that the stricter the parents are, the better the children turn out?	41	52	7
Arithmetic average	*34*	*55*	*11*

Table 4-9
Answers to Questions in Categories 1 and 2 According to Sex

	Men			Women		
	Rigidity (%)	Plasticity (%)	Don't Know (%)	Rigidity (%)	Plasticity (%)	Don't Know (%)
1. Does it annoy you to be told how to do things?	33	63	4	36	62	2
2. Do you always try to get your own way?	36	60	4	55	40	5

	Men			Women		
	Rigidity (%)	Plasticity (%)	Don't Know (%)	Rigidity (%)	Plasticity (%)	Don't Know (%)
3. If someone should show you that your way of life is not good, would you change?	23	32	14	26	64	10
4. Do you believe that many of your desires go against your moral and religious ideas?	59	35	5	72	19	9
5. If you are a man, do you feel that you are more of a man than others?	16	74	10	35	54	11
6. Do you believe that it is natural for married men to have mistresses?	22	67	11	16	74	10
7. Do you believe that men are more intelligent than women?	44	44	12	23	60	17
8. Do you believe that a dictatorship would be beneficial for Mexico?	33	55	12	20	47	33
9. If you believe in certain ideals, would you abandon them for the common good?	31	50	19	28	45	27
10. Do you believe that the stricter the parents are, the better the children turn out?	41	44	15	40	55	5
Arithmetic average	*34*	*56*	*11*	*35*	*52*	*13*

Table 4-10
Answers to Questions in Category 3 (Ability to See Projects
of Delayed Realization, "Reality Principle")

	Total Group		
	Rigidity (%)	Plasticity (%)	Don't Know (%)
1. Do you believe that Mexico should work out its own future without regard to other nations?	39	50	4
2. Would you be willing to give 1 percent of your annual income to increase the number of schools?	15	78	7

	Men			Women		
	Rigidity (%)	Plasticity (%)	Don't Know (%)	Rigidity (%)	Plasticity (%)	Don't Know (%)
3. If you believe in certain ideals, would you abandon them for the common good?				30	48	22
4. Do you believe that honest politicians are stupid?				17	76	7
5. Do you believe that someone who accepts a bribe is shrewd?				19	72	9
6. Do you believe that maids should work only eight hours a day?				21	65	14
Arithmetic average				24	65	10

Table 4-11
Answers to Questions in Category 3 According to Sex

	Men			Women		
	Rigidity (%)	Plasticity (%)	Don't Know (%)	Rigidity (%)	Plasticity (%)	Don't Know (%)
1. Do you believe that Mexico should work out its own future without regard to other nations?	52	41	7	34	49	17
2. Would you be willing to give 1 percent of your annual income to increase the number of schools?	17	76	7	9	80	11
3. If you believe in certain ideals, would you abandon them for the common good?	31	50	19	28	45	27
4. Do you believe that honest politicians are stupid?	24	78	3	6	81	13
5. Do you believe that someone who accepts a bribe is shrewd?	13	79	8	28	60	12
6. Do you believe that maids should work only eight hours a day?	24	64	12	16	66	18
Arithmetic average	27	64	9	20	64	16

Table 4-12
Answers to Questions in Category 4 (Incapacitating
or Distressing Mental Symptoms)

	Total Group		
	Rigidity (%)	Plasticity (%)	Don't Know (%)
1. Are you happier alone than in company?	21	76	3
2. Do you get angry frequently?	50	48	2
3. Do you think life is worth living?	14	74	12
4. Are you a nervous person?	52	45	3
5. Do you take offense easily?	46	46	8
6. Do you often feel very depressed?	44	53	3
7. Do you like the type of work with which you earn your living, or, if you are a housewife, do you like housework?	20	72	8
8. Do you get along better with friends than with members of your family?	32	64	4
9. Do you believe in trusting people?	68	22	10
10. Do you find it difficult to concentrate on what you read or study?	22	64	14
11. Do you frequently suffer from bile?	38	58	4
Arithmetic average	33	62	6

Table 4-13
Answers to Questions in Category 4 According to Sex

	Men			Women		
	Rigidity (%)	Plasticity (%)	Don't Know (%)	Rigidity (%)	Plasticity (%)	Don't Know (%)
1. Are you happier alone than in company?	12	82	0	26	66	8
2. Do you get angry frequently?	43	56	1	62	36	2
3. Do you think life is worth living?	12	77	11	18	69	13
4. Are you a nervous person?	43	52	5	66	33	1
5. Do you take offense easily?	43	51	6	51	40	9
6. Do you often feel very depressed?	34	64	2	57	41	2

	Men			Women		
	Rigidity (%)	Plasticity (%)	Don't Know (%)	Rigidity (%)	Plasticity (%)	Don't Know (%)
7. Do you like the type of work with which you earn your living?	27	68	5	9	80	11
8. Do you get along better with friends than with members of your family?	29	66	5	37	59	41
9. Do you believe in trusting people?	63	27	10	77	13	10
10. Do you find it difficult to concentrate on what you read or study?	21	68	11	24	58	18
11. Do you frequently suffer from bile?	28	66	6	52	47	1
Arithmetic average	32	62	6	44	49	7

Table 4-14
Answers to Questions in Category 5
(Inhibition of Behavior Provoked by Sociocultural Norms)

	Total Group		
	Rigidity (%)	Plasticity (%)	Don't Know (%)
1. Is your mother for you the dearest person in existence?	92	6	2
2. Do you believe that woman's place is in the home?	90	6	4
3. Do you believe that men should "wear the pants in the family"?	83	13	4
4. Do you believe it is proper for women to go out alone with men?	56	35	9
5. Do you believe that the stricter the parents are, the better the children turn out?	41	52	7
6. Do you believe that maids should organize in unions to improve their condition?	60	28	12
Arithmetic average	70	23	7

Table 4-15
Answers to Questions in Category 5 According to Sex

	Men			Women		
	Rigidity (%)	Plasticity (%)	Don't Know (%)	Rigidity (%)	Plasticity (%)	Don't Know (%)
1. Is your mother for you the dearest person in existence?	95	3	2	86	10	4
2. Do you believe that woman's place is in the home?	91	6	3	90	7	3
3. Do you believe that men should "wear the pants in the family"?	85	11	4	78	15	7
4. Do you believe it is proper for women to go out alone with men?	56	35	9	55	34	11
5. Do you believe that the stricter the parents are, the better the children turn out?	41	44	15	40	55	5
6. Do you believe that maids should organize in unions to improve their condition?	59	27	14	64	28	8
Arithmetic average	*71*	*21*	*8*	*69*	*25*	*6*

Table 4-16
Answers to Questions in Category 6 (Ignorance and Animism)

	Total Group		
	Rigidity (%)	Plasticity (%)	Don't Know (%)
1. Do you believe that a gift of five million pesos would solve all your problems?	42	47	11
2. Do you believe that black cats, broken mirrors, or certain numbers bring good or bad luck?	8	86	6
3. Do you believe that men are more intelligent than women?	36	50	14
4. Do you think that a dictatorship would be beneficial for Mexico?	28	52	20
5. If you believe in certain ideals, would you abandon them for the common good?	30	40	22

| | Total Group | | |
	Rigidity (%)	Plasticity (%)	Don't Know (%)
6. Do you believe that science can solve most human problems?	39	55	8
7. Do you believe that the stricter the parents are, the better the children turn out?	41	52	7
Arithmetic average	32	56	12

Table 4-17
Answers to Questions in Category 6 According to Sex

| | Men | | | Women | | |
	Rigidity (%)	Plasticity (%)	Don't Know (%)	Rigidity (%)	Plasticity (%)	Don't Know (%)
1. Do you believe that a gift of five million pesos would solve all your problems?	40	51	9	45	42	13
2. Do you believe that black cats, broken mirrors, or certain numbers bring good or bad luck?	6	90	4	11	80	9
3. Do you believe that men are more intelligent than women?	44	44	12	23	60	17
4. Do you think that a dictatorship would be beneficial for Mexico?	33	55	12	20	47	33
5. If you believe in certain ideals, would you abandon them for the common good?	31	50	19	28	45	27
6. Do you believe that science can solve most human problems?	36	57	7	44	46	10
7. Do you believe that the stricter the parents are, the better the children turn out?	41	44	15	40	55	5
Arithmetic average	33	56	11	30	54	16

APPENDIX 1

A Definition of Mental Health

As was indicated in the principal part of this work, it is believed that the concepts utilized are of value in the area of mental hygiene; some as an approximate measure of the level of mental health of individuals and groups; other as factors that take part directly in the production or prevention of mental illness. In this appendix the scientific foundation of each concept will be explained, and some sources from which the statement is derived will be briefly indicated.

Concept 1

The first concept is concerned with the level of ability of an individual or group to see, understand, and accept the points of view of other individuals or groups (related concept: tolerance).

The reader might ask: to what point does this ability correlate with the mental health of the individual who possesses it? It is thought that an individual capable of seeing the points of view of other individuals will almost necessarily be less exposed to conflicts with others. One of the fundamental concepts of psychopathology, accepted by clinical psychology as well as by experimental psychopathology, is that "conflict," that is, the presence of contradictions or of opposing impulses or needs, is the origin of maladjustment and mental illness. The great majority of psychiatrists, psychologists, and psychoanalysts will agree on this fundamental fact. In addition, experimental psychopathology has shown with "experimental neurosis" in man and animals that situations of conflict lead to psychopathologic reactions and symptoms of mental disturbance.[14] Another significant source of evidence in this area is found in the studies of general semantics.[15] "Reality" as a scientific concept is fully in accord with the idea of tolerance. Semantics has also shown that different points of view toward the same object or subject rarely contradict each other; semantics, we believe, can become one of the most powerful influences on mental hygiene,

[14] H. S. Liddell, "Conditioned Reflex Method and Experimental Neurosis," in *Personality and the Behavior Disorders*, ed. J. McV. Hunt; Neal E. Miller, "Experimental Studies of Conflict," in ibid.; Alexander R. Luria, *Nature of Human Conflicts*.

[15] Alfred Korzybski, *Science and Sanity: An Introduction to Non-Aristotelian Systems and General Semantics*; Wendell Johnson, *People in Quandaries*.

for it facilitates simple methods by means of which this ability to see, understand, and accept the points of view of other persons or groups can be highly developed.[16]

Concept 2

The second concept is that of the level of objectivity or impartiality with which individuals or groups "see" their own point of view or their needs or their actions (related concepts: objectification of the ego and avoidance of immoderate use of defense mechanisms).

Once more we confront the concept of conflict. An individual who scarcely knows his own motivational patterns—one, that is, who has no way or capacity to differentiate external reality from his own desires, who carries within himself mental maps that do not correspond to external territory—will almost certainly suffer undue conflict and frustration, both concepts of indubitable scientific value and proven capacity for the production of psychopathological symptoms.[17] Let us recall in passing that the majority of those who practice clinical psychology, whether psychiatrists, psychologists, or psychoanalysts, agree that the "objectification of the ego," whether they use this term for it or not, is an extremely important goal of psychotherapy.

Concept 3

The third concept is concerned with the level of ability to see, understand, and accept projects to be realized in the future that eventually redound to the material and spiritual benefit of the individual and of society (related concepts: ability to defer the satisfaction of impulses and needs—delay of reward; the Freudian reality principle).

This concept is quite clear for psychoanalysts. The Freudian reality principle that directs the judgments of the ego attempts precisely, as Ross Stagner would say, "to postpone an immediate pleasure in order to obtain a greater reward in the future or to avoid future pain."[18] The concept of delay of reward is related and experimental. It is understood that to live in society, in the ideal society in which each person "integrally" develops

[16] See S. I. Hayakawa, *Language in Action*; Irving J. Lee, *Language Habits in Human Affairs: An Introduction to General Semantics*; Kenneth S. Keyes, *How to Develop Your Thinking Ability*.

[17] John Dollard et al., *Frustration and Aggression*; Saul Rosenzweig, "An Outline of Frustration Theory," in *Personality and the Behavior Disorders*, ed. J. McV. Hunt; David C. McClelland and F. S. Apicella, "A Functional Classification of Verbal Reactions to Experimentally Induced Failure," *The Journal of Abnormal and Social Psychology* 40, no. 4 (1945).

[18] Ross Stagner, *Psychology of Personality*.

and enjoys his life without interfering with the integral development and enjoyment of others, it is of primary importance to encourage delay of reward, or the capacity to defer the satisfaction of impulses and desires.[19] The laboratory provides us with optimistic data in this regard: even dogs, monkeys, and white mice can learn to postpone satisfactions.[20] I believe that satisfactory methods, *not based on "irrational" authority,* can be developed as part of a program of mental hygiene for human beings, so that delay of reward will not be difficult. Another concept that can help to resolve the problems of society noted above is that of substitution of satisfaction; Kurt Lewin, through his experimental technique of interruption of tasks, has demonstrated this promising possibility in the human being.[21]

Concept 4

The fourth concept is that of the level of mental health, measured by the number of incapacitating or distressing symptoms.

There is little argument here. Symptoms of incapacity, mental disturbance, unhappiness are considered valid signs of maladjustment or mental illness. References are unnecessary.

Concept 5

The fifth concept deals with the level of inhibition of behavior (and of situations of conflict and frustration) provoked by sociocultural ideals and norms (related concept: the dynamic ego-superego).

It will be recognized that this concept is concerned above all with values. It implies the dynamic ego-superego accepted by most psychotherapists. But it is inevitably colored by the discussion of anthropo-sociocultural values that various psychoanalysts,[22] some psychiatrists,[23] and many psychologists[24] consider important. Basic to this inhibition of behavior are the

[19] With this concept we include those of avoidance conditioning and secondary reinforcement. See O. H. Mowrer and R. R. Lamoreaux, "Avoidance Conditioning and Signal Duration: A Study of Secondary Motivation and Reward," *Psychological Monographs* 54, no. 5 (1940).

[20] I. P. Pavlov, *Conditioned Reflexes;* J. B. Wolfe, "Effectiveness of Token-Rewards for Chimpanzees," *Comparative Psychological Monographs* 12, no. 6 (1936); O. H. Mowrer and A. D. Ullman, "Time as a Determinant in Integrative Learning," *Psychology Review* 52, no. 2 (1945).

[21] Kurt Lewin, *Dynamic Theory of Personality.*

[22] Abram Kardiner, *The Individual and His Society;* Karen Horney, *New Ways in Psychoanalysis;* Erich Fromm, *Man for Himself.*

[23] S. H. Kraines, *The Therapy of the Neuroses and Psychoses;* Harry Stack Sullivan, *Conceptions of Modern Psychiatry.*

[24] Werner Wolff, *Values and Personality;* Gordon W. Allport, *Personality: A*

concepts of conflict and frustration; these, we believe, are the fundamental concepts of psychopathology. Both, we have said, have been demonstrated in clinic and laboratory to be capable of provoking symptoms of mental disturbance. In Mexico there are a great many "values," or sociocultural ideals. Some seem to contribute to mental health (the compensatory mechanism of the fiesta, for example); others, however, seem to interfere with mental health. Let us take as an example the answer to the question "Is your mother for you the dearest person in existence?" We have considered a positive answer a sign of rigidity; let us explain. It should be recognized that the questionnaire is defective in asking for answers of "yes" or "no," when it is really more a matter of "up to a certain point" than of "yes" or "no." In any case, it is supposed that the person who answers affirmatively in general will enter into conflict when he or she has to establish new amorous relationships with sweetheart, husband or wife, child, etc. Unfortunately, each one of these persons can demand—and, it seems, does demand —to be the person who is loved most. This obviously provokes conflicts. Semanticists state that in reality each emotion is different from the next, and conflict is unnecessary if semantic teachings are fully followed. Nevertheless, this study is based on the present-day reactions of the Mexican, whose behavior in many ways is not guided by concepts of general semantics.

Replies of "yes" to this question also indicate that seemingly the individuals have a relationship with their mothers that can well produce the type of conflict, or rather complex,[25] that Freudians talk of, or at least that the Chicago school talks of: excessive dependence or emotional immaturity, etc.[26]

It would be appropriate to explain in this appendix the rational scientific foundation of each question; but, recognizing from the start that many of them are extraordinarily tentative, we will leave this effort for later.

Concept 6

The sixth concept is concerned with the level of ignorance and animism (related concept: the Korzybskian identification).

It is believed that, the less an individual knows of reality (his reality and external reality), the more exposed he will be to conflict and frustration

---

Psychological Interpretation; Gardner Murphy, *Personality: A Biosocial Approach.*

[25] By *complex* we mean a cluster of conflicts around an idea, the idea of *mother* or *authority*, for example.

[26] Franz Alexander and T. M. French, *Psychoanalytic Therapy*; Leon J. Saul, *Emotional Maturity.*

and thus to mental illness. *Ignorance* here does not mean ignorance of great cultural works, poetry, literature, philosophy, etc., but rather simple ignorance of internal and external reality, both understood in the framework of semantics.[27] Literature, poetry, philosophy (metaphysics), music, painting, and so on, are considered beautiful productions of enormous subjective value, but their application to daily life as maps of reality, instead of as lovely expressions of individual and subjective value, can lead to great confusion and catastrophes. It would be a case of confusing *what has value for me* with what has value in reality and for the majority. The extreme case of this confusion appears when an individual tries by force to impose on others something that he subjectively considers of great value: this is the case of dictators, fatal producers of misfortune.

Thus the opposite of ignorance is knowledge of facts that lead to less conflict and frustration for human beings. Semantics, already mentioned, produces techniques that will permit an important advance in this sense. The awareness of facts concerning the human personality, and the study of psychology and of the scientific social sciences, that is, the social sciences that rigorously use the scientific method, would be the next highly important steps in combatting this ignorance, an ignorance that leads to mental illness through maps that do not follow reality, thus naturally provoking frustration and conflict.

As for dictators, we should remember that the dictator is only the extreme case; the mental hygiene of nations demands that we investigate the intermediate cases that can produce the same catastrophes if they are not foreseen. Interesting studies of this problem are being carried out in the United States.[28] Nevertheless, we would like to add to this subject. If only we could learn not to confuse our evaluations of things with their objective values; this is one of man's serious problems. It is not difficult to understand this on certain levels—the artistic level, for example. Juan can say, "This is the most beautiful picture I have ever seen!" and Pedro can state, "What garbage!" Often both are aware that their evaluations are exclusively theirs and do not alter the painting in any way. But there has been and still is tremendous difficulty in other fields of evaluation. Mr. K, the final product of a given environment, with innate abilities X, with parents Z, with friends Y, educated in schools M and N, with religious beliefs R, and so on, comes to the conclusion that his values, those given to him "circumstantially" by his contacts, are the only valid ones. In his mind, perhaps through indoctrination, they are meaningful. Everything is fine up to this point; but suddenly he decides that these values (which he be-

[27] R. Díaz-Guerrero, "La semántica general de Korzybski," in *Memorias del Congreso Científico Mexicano*, XV, 531–535.

[28] T. W. Adorno et al., *The Authoritarian Personality*.

lieves to be important values and which therefore *are* important—to him) should be followed by the whole world. He then attempts to impose, in as many ways as he can, his own, intimate map of reality, without realizing that here he is confusing what has value for him with what has value in "reality": he really believes that his affirmations do change the picture! If his confusion is acute he will try, through all means, sometimes licit, sometimes brutal, to make the whole world follow his way of thinking. I hope that these words illustrate the need for individuals not to confuse their own evaluations, which can be studied and analyzed to discover their bases, with external reality, which changes in some respects from individual to individual, given the differing formulas of evaluation that each one has acquired. External reality is the reality valid for the majority, simply because it can be proven, can be demonstrated only through objective observations of events, through proof and counterproof, through reliability of prediction: that is, through the scientific method. It seems that, to make maps of external reality that will lead to provable and predictable facts, only the scientific method is adequate. On the other hand, the integral development of the personality (which should not of course be imposed on others, though culture can well be deeply admired: art, philosophy, literature, etc.) determines the great values that satisfy and develop the subjective life of individuals; but, we finally repeat, these values are not adequate maps of external reality, nor, therefore, methods to be followed in life if we want to exist in reality.

APPENDIX 2

The Tools of the Research

August, 1949

Good day:

You have been chosen as one of the five hundred people from among the two million inhabitants of Mexico City to have the privilege of answering the questionnaire that we enclose.

This is not a test of intelligence. Our purpose is to learn what the Mexican really thinks, feels, and desires, through Mexicans' own sincere opinions.

When you finish answering the questions, put the questionnaire in the accompanying envelope, seal it yourself, and give it to our representative. You are *not* asked to provide *your name* or *your address*, and your answers will be added to those of other people, so that you will remain completely anonymous.

Therefore, and since this is a scientific poll, we ask that your answers to the questions be completely open and unafraid.

Respectfully,

Guillermo Possidente, Bachelor of Psychology, Associate in Sciences
Rogelio Díaz-Guerrero, Physician and Surgeon, Doctor of Physiology and Psychology

IMPORTANT

As you know, there is a great difference between what one thinks he should do and what one really does; please answer these questions according to what you *really* think or what you would really do in most cases.

Thank you.

I. Do not give your name or address, but please answer the following questions:
1. Sex _____
2. Age _____
3. Occupation _____
4. Are you self-employed? _____
5. Do you work for others? _____
6. Marital status: Married: _____ Single: _____
     Widowed: _____ Divorced: _____
7. Did you go to school? _____
8. How many years did you complete? _____
9. How much do you earn per month? _____
10. If you have private means, what is your monthly income? _____

II. If you are a housewife, please answer these questions also:
1. What is your husband's occupation? _____
2. How much does your husband earn per month? _____

Answer each question "yes," "no," or "I don't know."

1. Are you happier alone than in company?
2. Is your mother for you the dearest person in existence?
3. Do you believe that a gift of five million pesos would solve all your problems?
4. Do you get angry frequently?
5. Do you think life is worth living?
6. Are you a nervous person?
7. Do you take offense easily?

8. Does it annoy you to be told how to do things?
9. Do you always try to get your own way?
10. Do you often feel very depressed?
11. If someone should show you that your way of life is not good, would you change?
12. *a.* Do you like the type of work with which you earn your living?
    b. If you are a housewife, do you like housework?
13. Do you get along better with friends than with members of your family?
14. Do you believe that black cats, broken mirrors, or certain numbers bring good or bad luck?
15. Do you believe in trusting people?
16. Do you think that many of your desires are contrary to your moral and religious ideas?
17. Do you find it difficult to concentrate on what you read or study?
18. *a.* If you are a man, do you feel that you are more of a man than others?
    b. If you are a woman, do you consider yourself very feminine?
19. Do you have confidence in yourself?
20. Do you frequently suffer from bile?
21. Do you believe that woman's place is in the home?
22. Do you believe that Mexico should work out its own future without regard to other nations?
23. Do you believe that it is necessary to cooperate with other nations?
24. Do you believe that most married men have mistresses?
25. Do you believe that it is natural for married men to have mistresses?
26. Would you be willing to give 1 percent of your annual income to increase the number of schools?
27. Do you believe that men are more intelligent than women?
28. Do you believe that a dictatorship would be beneficial for Mexico?
29. If you believe in certain ideals, would you abandon them for the common good?
30. Do you believe that someone who accepts a bribe is shrewd?
31. Do you believe that honest politicians are stupid?
32. Do you think that people who live according to the saying "Time is money" don't know how to enjoy life?
33. Do you believe that science can solve most human problems?
34. Do you believe that men should "wear the pants in the family"?
35. Do you believe it is proper for women to go out alone with men?
36. Do you believe that the stricter the parents are, the better the children turn out?

37. Do you think that the government should pass laws increasing the minimum salary?
38. Do you believe that maids should work only eight hours a day?
39. Do you believe that maids should organize in unions to improve their condition?
40. Do you think that people who earn less than three hundred pesos a month should pay taxes on what they earn?
41. Do you think that luxury items should be heavily taxed?
42. Do you think that workers ought to share in the earnings of the company for which they work?
43. Do you think that bus fares should be lowered to ten centavos?
44. Do you think that lawyers make too much money?
45. Do you think that tortillas and masa flour are very cheap?
46. Do you think that there are many things that you would very much like to have but cannot afford?

5. Two Core-Culture Patterns and the Diffusion of Values across Their Border

WITH ROBERT F. PECK

Introduction

The objective study of national character requires study of the values that influence important aspects of behavior. The objective study of values is, itself, no easy undertaking, but it may be facilitated by studying the same social phenomenon in two different cultures. The relevant values in each culture may thus be highlighted. Following this reasoning, a year or two ago we undertook a comparative study of the concept of "respect" in two different cultures: Mexico and the United States.

Respect was chosen for study because, along with love, authority,

NOTE. Reprinted from the *International Journal of Psychology*, 1967, vol. 2, pp. 275–282, by permission of the International Union of Psychological Science and Dunod Editeur, Paris.

The study was sponsored, in part, by the Hogg Foundation for Mental Health of the University of Texas and by CISAC of Monterrey, N.L. We are grateful for the cooperation of Lic. Raúl Pous Ortiz, director of the Escuela Nacional Preparatoria, and of the psychologists Olga Loredo, Oscar de la Rosa, Mario Cicero, Angel Vizcaíno, Roberto Moctezuma, Dr. Luis Gamiochipi, and Professor Rafael Navarro of the same institution.

friendship, and duty, it is one of the central motives that bind human society together. Moreover, there was some reason to believe that the relationship of respect takes a somewhat different form, different ways of feeling and acting, in the United States and in Latin America. Although the Spanish word *respeto* and the English word *respect* are identical in origin, very similar in form, and similar in dictionary definition, the actual behavior patterns and the conceptual associations surrounding these terms might, we thought, differ significantly in the two cultures.

First, we compared two centers rather far removed from one another: Mexico City and Austin, Texas. Recently, however, with the aid and encouragement of colleagues in Monterrey, Mexico, and Edinburg, Texas, data from those border areas have made it possible to investigate the possibility of a mutual diffusion of values in the transition zone between the two societies. Numerous facts suggest that such diffusion should be observable. Historically, Texas was first settled from Mexico. The influence of that Mexican heritage is still pronounced in the Rio Grande Valley of Texas, where Edinburg is located, and as far north as San Antonio. Ever since, migration across the border has continued in both directions. Currently, many Mexicans work and travel in the United States, while many Americans participate in businesses in Mexico, especially in Monterrey. Indeed, in other parts of Mexico, the people of Monterrey are sometimes regarded as the "Yankees of Mexico." Similarly, South Texas has an aura of Old Mexico about it for most people in the United States.

Population

Partly because they were accessible and cooperative, but also because they represent the future leaders and opinion makers of their societies, college students were selected for study. If anything, similarities might be expected in their intellectual orientation and in their social background that transcend national differences. Thus, any value differences found are likely to be genuine; and greater differences might be expected if noncollege populations were compared.

Seven different groups were distinguished and separately treated in the analysis: (*a*) liberal arts students at the National University

Table 5-1
Subject-Sample Sizes

Group	Males	Females	Total
Texas, education majors	36	228	264
Texas, Arts and Sciences	176	164	340
Edinburg, Anglo	100	99	199
Edinburg, Latin	100	99	199
Monterrey	114	87	200
Mexico City, liberal arts	216	82	298
Mexico City, normal school	114	200	314
Totals	856	958	1,814

of Mexico; (*b*) students preparing to be secondary-school teachers at a normal school near Mexico City; (*c*) students at Monterrey Technological Institute and at a girls' college in Monterrey; (*d*) students of Mexican descent at Pan American College in Edinburg, Texas; (*e*) Anglo-American students at Pan American College; (*f*) students in the College of Arts and Sciences at the University of Texas; and (*g*) students taking an education course at The University of Texas. The numbers of each sex in each group are shown in Table 5-1.

Students at the National University are drawn from all over Mexico; so that sample undoubtedly included some people from the northern states of Mexico. Similarly, students come to the University of Texas from all over the state, as well as from many other parts of the United States. Some in this study undoubtedly came from border areas near Mexico, although this was not checked. Such factors would tend to reduce the differences between the University of Mexico and the University of Texas samples and between these samples and the border samples from Monterrey and Edinburg.

Procedure

A check-list was constructed, made up of twenty different possible meanings that might be associated with the term *respect*. This questionnaire was first composed in English; then an exact counterpart was prepared in Spanish. We strove for semantically identical meanings, which were not always the same as linguistically literal translations. The English version was administered to the Austin and Edinburg samples. The Spanish version was used in Monterrey and Mexico City.

The English version of the questionnaire reads as follows:

INSTRUCTIONS: The word "respect" has several important meanings. Not everybody uses the word in the same way. Below is a list of 20 different ways in which the word "respect" might conceivably be used. Please place a check mark in front of those statements that seem to you to represent appropriate uses of the word "respect." Where a statement does not fit the meaning of "respect," leave the space blank.

1. To look up to somebody with admiration.
2. To look up to somebody with awe.
3. To fear somebody.
4. To love somebody.
5. To be willing to treat someone else on an equal footing.
6. To give someone else a chance.
7. To feel affection.
8. To feel admiration for somebody.
9. To anticipate a certain degree of protection from the respected person.
10. To anticipate the possibility of punishment from the respected person.
11. To feel a certain degree of protectiveness toward the respected person.
12. To dislike somebody.
13. To keep from trespassing on somebody else's rights.
14. To feel you like to obey someone.
15. To feel you have to obey someone, whether you like it or not.
16. To feel it is your duty to obey someone.
17. To be considerate of somebody else's feelings.
18. To be considerate of somebody else's ideas.
19. Not to invade somebody else's privacy.
20. To avoid interfering in somebody else's life.

After all samples were completed, an F-test was applied to determine whether any one sample consistently tended to check a larger or smaller total number of items. There was no significant response bias in any sample; so a direct comparison of percentages of response to each item in the questionnaire was possible for all samples.[1]

[1] The reader who is not interested in the technical, statistical aspects of the

Table 5-2
Analysis of Variance for Item 1: An Illustration

Item 1: Admiration

Source	SS	df	MS	F
Total	216.08	1,399	.15	—
Between cells	27.49	13	2.11	15.54[a]
Groups	24.89	6	4.15	30.49[a]
Linear (L)	22.57	1	22.57	165.90[a]
Quadratic (Q)	1.05	1	1.05	7.73[a]
UT-Ed. vs. UT-A&S	.72	1	.72	5.31[b]
Sex	1.32	1	1.32	9.71[a]
Groups by sex	1.27	6	.21	1.56
Linear (L)	.59	1	.59	4.35[b]
Quadratic (Q)	.15	1	.15	1.11
UT-Ed. vs. UT-A&S	.06	1	.06	.46
Within cells	188.59	1,386	.13	—

SS: sum of squares
df: degree of freedom
MS: mean square
F: F-test.
UT-Ed.: education students at the University of Texas
UT-A&S: students in the College of Arts and Sciences, University of Texas
[a] $p < .01$.
[b] $p < .05$.

Table 5-2 illustrates the statistical analysis that was applied to
each item. Analysis of variance was done on the 1604 computer at
the University of Texas, using a program written especially for this
study by Dr. Donald Veldman. Line L in Table 5-2 shows whether
there is a significant linear effect differentiating the seven samples in
a single direction, as from the UT Arts and Sciences sample at one
end, through the "border" samples, to Mexico City at the other end.
The Q line shows whether the Edinburg Latin and Monterrey
groups, combined, differ significantly from their "neighbor" groups
of Edinburg Anglos and Mexico City students. Table 5-3 here shows

---

analysis may skip the following paragraph and resume reading under the heading
"Results," where the findings are explained.

Table 5-3
Percentages

	UT-Ed.	UT-A&S	ED-Ang.	ED-Mex.	MTY	MC-Prep.	MC-Norm.	Totals
Males	92.0	86.0	89.0	89.0	80.0	60.0	49.0	77.85
Females	98.0	87.0	96.0	85.0	88.0	68.0	66.0	84.00
Totals	95.0	86.5	92.5	87.0	84.0	64.0	57.5	

UT-Ed.: education students at the University of Texas
UT-A&S: students in the College of Arts and Sciences, University of Texas
ED-Ang.: Anglo-American students at Pan American College, Edinburg
ED-Mex.: students of Mexican descent at Pan American College, Edinburg
MTY: preparatory-school students in Monterrey
MC-Prep.: preparatory-school students in Mexico City
MC-Norm.: normal-school students in Mexico City

the total percentage of response to the item by men and by women, in each group.

Results

The core-culture patterns. With the exception of one item, one or another person in every group checked each item. (No University of Texas men checked item 12, "dislike," as a possible meaning of *respect.*) Thus, differences among the groups are a matter of degree, not of total dissimilarity. Nonetheless, the analysis of variance showed that there were significant differences among the seven groups on nineteen of the twenty items.

In order to establish a picture of the "core value pattern" in the two societies, first, Table 5-4 was constructed. It shows that the University of Texas students picked six items (1, 5, 6, 8, 17, 18) significantly more often than did the students in the Mexico City area. The Mexican students, significantly more often than the Austin students, checked the following items: 4, 7, 9, 11, 12, 13, 15, 16, 20. In addition, items 2 and 3 were checked much more often by the Monterrey sample than by the University of Texas sample; hence they may marginally be considered as part of the Mexican constellation.

Reading the items in the two halves of Table 5-4, an interesting contrast in relationship patterns appears. The "American" pattern

Table 5-4
Respect: The "Core-Culture" Pattern in Mexico and in Texas

United States (University of Texas)	Mexico
1. Look up to with admiration	
	2. Awe (Monterrey only)
	3. Fear (Monterrey only)
	4. Love
5. Treat as an equal	
6. Give the other a chance	
	7. Affection
8. Admire	
	9. Expect protection from
	11. Feel protective toward
	12. Dislike
	13. Don't trespass on rights
	15. Have to obey, like it or not
	16. Duty to obey
17. Consider other's feelings	
18. Consider other's ideas	
	20. Don't interfere in other's life

("Texan" would be a more safely limited term) depicts the respect relationship as one between equals. One can admire and look up to another person, it seems, perhaps for some specific attribute, without feeling generally inferior or subordinate. Indeed, there is a suggestion of calmly confident self-assurance in the emphasis on giving the other person a chance and being considerate of his feelings and his ideas. Much less often than the Mexicans do Texas students associate respect with the idea of obedience or protection; and they rarely connect it with fear or dislike. In fact, in general, the respect relationship is less laden with intense, personal emotion for the Texas students. While the difference is only one of degree, there seems to be a consistent overall pattern of relatively detached, democratic give-and-take among equals, when the Texans picture the respect relationship.

The Mexican pattern looks equally self-consistent and quite different. It pictures respect as an extremely intimate relationship, involving a good deal of strong personal feeling. For some, part of this feeling is negative, in opposition to the very positive emotions of love and affection that are also expressed. Reciprocal protectiveness is another major theme. Finally, there is considerable concern about not interfering in the other person's life or trespassing on his rights—perhaps a more immediate danger when life is so close, emotion-laden, and so intimately bound up. The overall pattern tends to be on the authoritarian model. Most of the Mexicans think that respect involves a positive duty to obey; and a third to half of them, unlike most American students, feel that respect means you have to obey the respected person, whether you like it or not. Thus, in contrast to the American pattern, most of the Mexicans portray the respect relationship as an intricate web of reciprocal duties and dependencies, cast in a hierarchical mold, with strong feelings of emotional involvement to support it and, sometimes, to strain it.

Diffusion of values in the border zone. Upon complete analysis of all seven groups' responses, a number of interesting phenomena appeared in the groups from the border areas. The several different item-patterns are summarized in Table 5-5, under headings which can only be speculative, but which seem reasonable.

Group I consists of five items where the significant dividing line, in response frequencies, falls between the Anglo-American samples and the Mexican or Mexican-descended samples. All five stems were part of the "typically Mexican" pattern described above and in Table 5-4. This cluster is tentatively designated as the set of culture-typed values. It places emphasis on obedience, expectation of protection, concern not to invade the respected one's rights, and affection for that person. The Mexican-Americans in Edinburg retain these Mexican values.

Group II includes six items on which the Mexican-Americans in Edinburg respond like the Anglo-Americans there and in Austin, and all differ significantly from the Mexican nationals. On these "typically American" values of equality, considerateness, admiration, and almost never dislike, it might be said that the Mexican-American students in this border area have acculturated to the American pattern on these points.

Table 5-5
Diffusion of Values

I. "Culture-typed" values 7. Affection 9. Expect protection from 13. Avoid trespassing on rights 15. Have to obey, like it or not 16. Duty to obey	Mexicans, in Mexico and United States
II. "National" values 5. Treat as equal 6. Give someone a chance 8. Feel admiration 12. (Not) dislike 17. Consider feelings 18. Consider ideas	United States, including Mexican-Americans in Edinburg, who are perhaps acculturated to U.S. pattern on these points
III. "Diffused" values 4. To love 11. Protective toward 20. Avoid interfering in their life	Mexicans, and also Edinburg Anglos, who are perhaps acculturated to the Mexican pattern on these points
1. Look up with admiration	United States, but shared by Monterrey people, who are possibly acculturated to the U.S. view on this point
IV. "Border" effect 2. Look up with awe 3. Fear	Monterrey (especially women), but not Austin or Mexico City
10. Expect punishment from 14. Like to obey	Edinburg and Monterrey, but not Austin or Mexico City

Considering the differences and even the implicit contradictions between the values in Group I and Group II, both of which the Edinburg Mexican-Americans hold, it would scarcely be surprising if they experience some of the same personal and social conflicts as members of other national groups who have migrated to the United States. Whatever their historical generation, they seem to be facing the "second-generation" problem of acculturation.

The next cluster of items suggests that there has been two-way diffusion of values on both sides of the border, even in the very restricted area tapped by this study. On the "Mexican" meaning of respect: to love, to feel protective toward, to avoid interfering, the Edinburg Anglos resemble the Mexicans significantly more than they do the U.S. samples. Perhaps they have acculturated to the Mexican view of life on these points, and admirable points they are. Conversely, on the admiration item, the Monterrey students resemble those in the United States more than those in Mexico City; acculturation, possibly?

Finally, there are two sets of items that show a unique pattern: they are chosen much more often by people in one of the border samples than by the "core" samples in either Mexico City or Austin. Only in Monterrey do an appreciable number of students associate respect with awe and with fear. In Edinburg and Monterrey there is also a significantly higher incidence of votes for "expecting punishment" and "liking to obey." There is almost a sadomasochistic aura about this set of items. Could it be another bit of evidence for acculturative stress in a border zone? Perhaps, but that must remain speculation, pending more data. In any case, whether it is due to acculturative effects or to some quite different cause, on these points the "core" U.S. and "core" Mexican samples resemble each other more than they do the border samples.

Summary and Conclusion

Using a questionnaire about various possible meanings of *respect*, in parallel Spanish and English forms, two "core-culture patterns" were discovered, one typifying students in Mexico City; the other, students at the University of Texas. The American pattern was a relatively detached, self-assured equalitarianism. The Mexican pattern was one of close-knit, highly emotionalized, reciprocal dependence and dutifulness, within a firmly authoritarian framework.

When samples from the border zone (Monterrey, Mexico, and Edinburg, Texas) were added, the response-similarity analysis suggested considerable diffusion of values in the border area. The largest effect appeared to be an assimilative semiacculturation of Mexican-Americans in Edinburg to the "American" pattern. But there was also evidence suggesting certain acculturations of border Anglo-Americans to Mexican values. A curious phenomenon also turned up: a "border effect," wherein people on one or both sides of the border were more different from either "core-culture pattern" than the core patterns were from each other.

It cannot be overemphasized that some U.S. students' answers were the same as the Mexicans', and vice versa. The differences shown in Tables 5-4 and 5-5 are no more than differences in the modal patterns of the two culture groups. They are real differences, nonetheless; and they do resemble other descriptions of the two cultures. If the present findings have any value, it is less for their limited depth than for the fact that they are entirely objective in nature and for the fascinating questions they raise. They point, rather specifically, to lines for further, more sophisticated research.

The general method developed for this research is readily usable in other regions or countries. It can be used where more complex forms of data gathering are unmanageable; and it is adapted for analysis of large numbers of cases by high-speed computer. As a large-scale survey method, therefore, to be supplemented by depth techniques in selected small samples, it offers useful promise for cross-cultural studies of several kinds. Within its limitations, it provides a totally objective way of comparing the values of people from two or more cultures and thus of measuring the similarity or difference of the cultures. In the present instance, it furnished an illuminating initial probe into certain culturally differentiated values and into certain facets of national character in Mexico and the United States. It could, of course, be used to measure many kinds of values, such as achievement drive, economic values, affiliation, and others.

6. Respect and Status in Two Cultures

WITH ROBERT F. PECK

A number of different studies have shown that there is a definite difference in interpersonal expectations and in interpersonal interaction, within the family as well as within society itself, between the Mexican and American cultures.

The data reported by Díaz-Guerrero show the clear tendency in Mexican culture to give supremacy to the man and the clear tendency of the woman toward self-sacrifice. Díaz-Guerrero has also compared certain Mexican and American sociocultural presuppositions concerning interpersonal relationships.[1]

NOTE. This essay was originally published as "Respeto y posición social en dos culturas," in *Proceedings of the 7th Interamerican Congress of Psychology* 2 (1967): 79–88.

The study was sponsored, in part, by the Hogg Foundation for Mental Health at the University of Texas and by CISAC of Monterrey, N.L.

The essay has been translated by Cecile C. Wiseman.

[1] See Essay 1 in this volume and the following works by R. Díaz-Guerrero: "Mexican Assumptions about Interpersonal Relations," *ETC.: A Review of General Semantics* 16, no. 2 (Winter 1959): 185–188; and "Differences in Mexican and U.S. National Character and Their Implications for Public Health Practice" (paper presented at the Hidalgo Conference, Edinburg, Texas).

Among many other interesting facts, the work of H. H. Anderson and G. L. Anderson—published as well as unpublished—shows that American children expect nonauthoritarian interpersonal relationships with older people, while Mexican children frequently expect and easily fit into authoritarian relationships with their elders.[2]

In a series of anthropological studies, W. Madsen, O. I. Romano, and Arthur J. Rubel refer from time to time to concepts like *donism* (cultivation of the *don*, a title of respect), respect for the aged, predominance of the male, etc., in the subculture formed by the Mexican-Americans.[3]

Recently we have undertaken a series of studies that deal with the interpersonal relationship known as *respect* and have investigated it in samples of Mexicans and Americans.[4] We have found that Mexican and American students of equivalent age, sex, academic level, and type of academic education conceptualize the idea of respect in extraordinarily different form. Thus, on a scale of twenty questions designed to elicit their conceptions of respect, in seventeen cases the Mexican and American subjects differ to a statistically significant degree. The implications of the term *respect*, then, are quite different in the two cultures. The next step, which concerns us now, deals with the relationship that exists between respect and that

[2] H. H. Anderson and G. L. Anderson, "Cultural Reactions to Conflict, a Study of Adolescent Children in Four Countries: Germany, England, Mexico, United States," *The Journal of Social Psychology* 50 (1959): 47–55; idem, "Cultural Reactions to Conflict: A Study of Adolescent Children in Seven Countries," in *Psychological Approaches to Intergroup and International Understanding: A Symposium of the Third Interamerican Congress of Psychology*, ed. G. M. Gilbert, pp. 27–32; idem, "A Cross-National Study of Teacher-Child Relations as Reported by Adolescent Children" (document presented at the Quinto Congreso Interamericano de Psicología, Mexico City, December, 1957); idem, "Symposium on Culture Components as a Significant Factor in Child Development: Image of the Teacher by Adolescent Children in Seven Countries," *American Journal of Orthopsychiatry* 31, no. 3 (1961): 481–492.

[3] W. Madsen, *Society and Health in the Lower Rio Grande Valley*; O. I. Romano, "Donship in a Mexican-American Community in Texas," *American Anthropologist* 62, no. 6 (1960): 966–976; Arthur J. Rubel, "Concepts of Disease in Mexican-American Culture," *American Anthropologist* 62, no. 5 (1960): 795–814.

[4] See Essay 5.

interesting sociopsychological construct called *status*. This interesting hybrid of self-esteem and social interpersonal interaction has been considered as a good measurement of what societies and cultures have traditionally defined as desirable.

Therefore, although we know now that respect has different meanings in the societies that we are examining, we can depart from the somewhat obvious hypothesis that in both societies the person who receives respect increases, by this fact alone, his status within the society.

Transcultural exploration of the relationship between respect and status can be an important avenue toward developing an understanding of problems of international sociology, such as the very interesting one encountered by Dr. S. Thomas Lagner. Dr. Lagner studied groups of women in New York, Mexico City, and Tehuantepec, in an attempt to prove or disprove the hypothesis that social status is positively related to the decrease of neurotic symptoms of a hypochondriac nature.[5] Starting from the Díaz-Guerrero studies, he thought that, given the low social status of the Mexican woman, as compared to the American woman, and given also the striking exception to this rule exemplified by the women of Tehuantepec, he could easily obtain data that would permit him to prove or disprove his hypothesis. In general the results of his study supported his thesis, but he was surprised and perplexed by the fact that there was no relation, particularly in Mexico City, between most of the statements of the women in favor of equality with men and the number of their symptoms. In correspondence with Dr. Lagner, one of us (Díaz-Guerrero) suggested to him, before obtaining the results of the present study, that the solution to the puzzle could be found in the fact that the affirmations of attitudes of equality with men—as shown in the American socioculture—could well be unrelated to an increase in status within the Mexican socioculture. The present study does in fact show that respect—an increase in social prestige or status—can be accorded the Mexican women simply for their age, or because they are mothers, or simply *because they are women*; it

[5] S. Thomas Lagner, "Psychophysiological Symptoms and Women's Status in Two Mexican Communities." Unpublished.

can even be inferred from the facts reported in this study that the improvement in status derived from the earlier attitudes of the socio-culture can easily come into conflict with improvements in status derived from attitudes favoring equality.

Sociologists, who, as Leonard Broom says,[6] are becoming more and more interested in the study and application of scientific con-structs, such as consistency of status or status crystallization, might be surprised at the use we are making here of the concept of status. Nevertheless, although they usually define status by criteria of occu-pation, level of education, ethnic group, etc., I do not believe that they will be opposed to the use—in transcultural studies—of the idea, concept, and practice of respect as a criterion of social status. It is even possible to speculate about the relation that respect bears to that complex construct that the sociologist calls *consistency of status*. Our plan, in this study, is to analyze the frequency with which students from the Mexican and American cultures, male and female, consider certain attributes of individuals and certain roles that they play as worthy of respect. We assume, in addition, for the obvious importance implied in the assumption, that one who receives respect in a society automatically acquires status or a certain level of "social position" in that society.

Methodology

This study is based on the answers given to a questionnaire by 298 Mexican students and 340 American students. The Mexican sample consisted of 298 students from preparatory schools, including 216 men and 82 women. The American subjects were drawn from the first and second years of the College of Arts and Sciences of the University of Texas, and the group was composed of 176 men and 164 women. The average ages of both groups were similar, and the academic programs of the compared groups were also as similar as they can be in the two cultures.

The following questionnaire was used, consisting of a list of sixty

[6] Leonard Broom, "Social Differentiation and Stratification," in *Sociology Today: Problems and Prospects*, ed. Robert K. Merton, Leonard Broom, and Leonard S. Cottrell, Jr., pp. 429–441.

different types of "roles," such as professional activities, educational activities, roles played within the family or civil or religious institutions, and personal attributes, such as age, sex, and so on.

INSTRUCTIONS: Below is a list of many different kinds of people. Toward some, you probably will think it appropriate to use the word "respect." Toward others, you may think it inappropriate. Place a check-mark in front of the people to whom the word "respect" might apply. Leave all others blank.

1.	your equals	31.	your bosses
2.	people that work under you	32.	your teachers
3.	your classmates	33.	your father
4.	your mother	34.	your older brother(s)
5.	your younger brother(s)	35.	your older sister(s)
6.	your younger sister(s)	36.	the policeman
7.	old men	37.	old women
8.	middle-aged men	38.	middle-aged women
9.	young men	39.	young women
10.	teen-age boys	40.	teen-age girls
11.	young boys	41.	young girls
12.	baby boys	42.	baby girls
13.	older male cousins	43.	older female cousins
14.	younger male cousins	44.	younger female cousins
15.	uncles	45.	aunts
16.	grandfathers	46.	grandmothers
17.	priests	47.	ministers
18.	older male friends	48.	older female friends
19.	younger male friends	49.	younger female friends
20.	older male neighbors	50.	older female neighbors
21.	younger male neighbors	51.	younger female neighbors
22.	the constitution	52.	wealthy people
23.	middle-class people	53.	poor people
24.	low-class people	54.	beggars
25.	lawyers	55.	doctors
26.	engineers	56.	actors
27.	artists	57.	philosophers
28.	writers	58.	intellectuals
29.	musicians	59.	skilled workers
30.	laborers	60.	servants

This questionnaire has been developed by Dr. Robert F. Peck of The University of Texas and Dr. Rogelio Díaz-Guerrero of The National University of Mexico.

Using this questionnaire the reader can carry out an interesting test of his knowledge of his own socioculture. Before each of the sixty items of the questionnaire he can write in the letters *HR*, if he believes that in the United States the individuals or roles described receive high respect; the letters *MR*, if he believes that they receive medium respect; and the letters *LR*, if he believes that they receive little respect. Then he can compare his results with those obtained in the present study and can rate his knowledge of American socioculture in this area. Thus, if he agrees on fifteen or fewer items, his knowledge will be poor. If he agrees in sixteen to thirty cases, it will be average. If he agrees on forty-five to sixty items, it will be very good. Naturally, the reader ought to compare his or her answers to those of American men or women, according to his or her sex. The reader can also examine his knowledge of the Mexican socioculture, answering the questionnaire as he believes a Mexican student would, and then comparing his answers with the actual results and once again tabulating as above his level of knowledge.

Analysis of Results

In order to make the results of this transcultural comparison clearly comprehensible, we have decided to proceed in the following form. First we will present the results obtained in the Mexican culture, in order to obtain an overview of what types of human characteristics and roles merit respect in this culture. Next, exactly the same type of analysis will be carried out with the results obtained from the American culture, and, finally, a transcultural comparison will be made to bring out the differences. In order to carry out this program with the greatest possible validity and clarity, we have done two things with the results. First, we have classified the results into various categories; and, second, we have made a decision about how to quantify the gradation of respect within both cultures. Since we found a great variation in the frequencies of affirmative responses for each of the items of the questionnaire, and since there is no pre-established criterion for classifying these frequencies of affirmative responses, we decided to divide the items into three large categories: (*a*) items that were answered affirmatively by significantly more than 50 percent of the subjects; (*b*) items that were answered affirmatively by half or approximately half of the subjects; (*c*) items that were answered affirmatively by significantly less than 50 percent of the subjects. To establish the statistical differences of these three groups we used the statistic Chi square.

Let us look now at Table 6-1 and explain how it charts what we can call the "cosmos of respect" in Mexican society.[7]

Beneath the title of the table, in the center, is written Qualitative Categories, and immediately below this phrase are the different qualitative categories that we have taken into account in the study. From left to right, these categories are age and sex, immediate family, collateral family, friends, neighbors, occupations, economic position, and miscellaneous items. On the upper left side of the table is written Quantitative Categories, referring to the divisions *high respect, medium respect,* and *little respect.* Thus, if we want to know the level of respect received according to age and sex, we will look in the column beneath Age, Sex, and we will find that those who receive high respect are old men, old women, middle-aged women, young women, teen-age girls, and middle-aged men. Descending vertically, we see that those who receive medium respect are young men and baby girls; and, continuing vertically to the bottom, those who receive little respect in Mexican society are young boys, teen-age boys, and baby boys. In this same way we can observe the degree of respect received by the immediate family, all of whom, as can be seen, receive high respect. One can also observe what happens with collateral family, with friends, with neighbors, with different occupations, with economic position, and with the miscellaneous items. Tables 6-2–6-4 are all read in the same way as Table 6-1, which refers to the "cosmos of respect," as perceived by male Mexican students. Table 6-2 shows the cosmos of respect as perceived by male students in American society; Table 6-3 shows the cosmos of respect

[7] Remember that this cosmos of respect has been obtained by a fairly representative sample of second-year students of the Escuela Nacional Preparatoria de México. Remember, then, that this is their vision of respect; but remember too that students in general have the clearest minds and that their vision of the cosmos of respect in Mexican culture could well be the most objective perception possible of the Mexican socioculture in this respect.

Table 6-1
Cosmos of Respect in Mexican Society (Male Preparatory Students)

Quantitative Categories	Qualitative Categories							
	Age, Sex	Immediate Family	Collateral Family	Friends	Neighbors	Occupations	Economic Position	Miscellaneous Items
High respect	Old men Old women Middle-aged women Young women Teen-age girls Middle-aged men	Mother Father Older brother Older sister Younger sister Younger brother	Grandfathers Grandmothers Aunts Uncles Older female cousins Younger female cousins Older male cousins	Older female friends Younger female friends Older male friends	Older male neighbors Older female neighbors	Teachers Priests Bosses Doctors Policemen Philosophers Intellectuals Engineers Lawyers Writers Laborers Ministers Servants Skilled workers Musicians	Middle-class people Poor people Low-class people Beggars	The constitution People that work under you Classmates Equals
						Artists Actors	Wealthy people	
Medium respect	Young men Baby girls		Younger male cousins	Younger male friends	Younger female neighbors			
Little respect	Young boys Teen-age boys Baby boys				Younger male neighbors			

NOTE. Within each quantitative category, the items of this table and the following ones have been arranged from top to bottom in a hierarchy that goes from those most frequently chosen to those least frequently chosen by the subjects. Verifications using Chi square have demonstrated that the quantitative categories—high, medium, and little respect—are real and distinct. The level of significance varied for the individual items from .05 to much higher levels of significance, such as .01, .001, .0001, etc.

Table 6-2

Cosmos of Respect in American Society (Male Undergraduate Students)

Quantitative Categories	Qualitative Categories							
	Age, Sex	Immediate Family	Collateral Family	Friends	Neighbors	Occupations	Economic Position	Miscellaneous Items
High respect	Old women Old men Middle-aged men Middle-aged women Young women Young men	Mother Father Older brother Older sister Younger brother Younger sister	Grandmothers Grandfathers Aunts Uncles Older female cousins Older male cousins	Older female friends Older male friends Younger female friends	Older female neighbors Older male neighbors	Teachers Ministers Priests Doctors Bosses Intellectuals Lawyers Policemen Writers Engineers Philosophers Artists Skilled workers Musicians	Middle-class people	Equals People that work under you Classmates The constitution
Medium respect	Teen-age girls		Younger female cousins Younger male cousins	Younger male friends	Younger female neighbors	Actors Laborers Servants	Poor people Low-class people Wealthy people	
Little respect	Teen-age boys Young girls Young boys Baby girls Baby boys				Younger male neighbors		Beggars	

Table 6-3

Cosmos of Respect in Mexican Society (Female Preparatory Students)

Quantitative Categories	Qualitative Categories							
	Age, Sex	Immediate Family	Collateral Family	Friends	Neighbors	Occupations	Economic Position	Miscellaneous Items
High respect	Old women Old men Middle-aged men Middle-aged women	Mother Father Older brother Older sister	Grandfathers Uncles Aunts Grandmothers Older male cousins Older female cousins	Older female friends Older male friends	Older male neighbors Older female neighbors	Teachers Bosses Priests Policemen Philosophers Doctors Writers Intellectuals Engineers Laborers Lawyers Musicians Skilled workers	Middle-class people Poor people Low-class people	The constitution People that work under you Classmates
Medium respect	Young men Young women Teen-age boys Teen-age girls	Younger sister Younger brother	Younger female cousins Younger male cousins			Servants Ministers Actors Artists	Wealthy people Beggars	Equals
Little respect	Young girls Young boys Baby girls Baby boys			Younger female friends Younger male friends	Younger male neighbors Younger female neighbors			

Table 6-4

Cosmos of Respect in American Society (Female Undergraduate Students)

Quantitative Categories	Qualitative Categories							
	Age, Sex	Immediate Family	Collateral Family	Friends	Neighbors	Occupations	Economic Position	Miscellaneous Items
High respect	Old men Old women Middle-aged men Middle-aged women Young men Young women	Mother Father Older brother Older sister Younger sister	Grandfathers Grandmothers Uncles Aunts Older female cousins Older male cousins	Older male friends Older female friends	Older male neighbors Older female neighbors	Priests Teachers Ministers Doctors Lawyers Intellectuals Policemen Writers Engineers Philosophers Musicians Artists Skilled workers	Middle-class people	Equals The constitution Classmates People that work under you
Medium respect		Younger brother	Younger female cousins Younger male cousins	Younger male friends Younger female friends	Younger male neighbors Younger female neighbors	Laborers Servants Actors	Poor people	
Little respect	Teen-age boys Teen-age girls Young boys Young girls Baby girls Baby boys						Low-class people Wealthy people Beggars	

Table 6-5
Transcultural Comparison
Male Preparatory Students in Mexico and Male Undergraduates in the United States

	Mexico +/− R	Mexico Q.C.	United States +/− R	United States Q.C.
Age and sex				
Old men	+	HR	—	HR
Young men	—	MR	+	HR
Young boys	+	LR	—	LR
Baby boys	+	LR	—	LR
Young women	+	HR	—	HR
Teen-age girls	+	HR	—	MR
Young girls	+	HR	—	LR
Baby girls	+	MR	—	LR
Friends				
Older male friends	—	HR	+	HR
Economic position				
Middle-class people	+	HR	—	HR
Low-class people	+	HR	—	HR
Poor people	+	HR	—	MR
Wealthy people	+	MR	—	MR
Beggars	+	HR	—	LR

	Mexico +/− R	Mexico Q.C.	United States +/− R	United States Q.C.
Immediate family				
Older brothers	+	HR	—	HR
Older sisters	+	HR	—	HR
Younger sisters	+	HR	—	HR
Neighbors				
Miscellaneous items				
The constitution	+	HR	—	HR
Equals	—		+	

	Mexico +/− R	Mexico Q.C.	United States +/− R	United States Q.C.
Collateral family				
Grandfathers	+	HR	—	HR
Uncles	+	HR	—	HR
Aunts	+	HR	—	HR
Younger female cousins	+	HR	—	HR
Occupations				
Laborers	+	HR	—	MR
Servants	+	HR	—	MR
Ministers	—	HR	+	HR

+ or — R: more or less respect in the given culture, as compared to the other culture

Q.C.: quantitative category of respect

HR: high respect

MR: medium respect

LR: little respect

The cultural differences shown are statistically significant by proof of Chi square and to a level of 0.05 or more.

according to the statements of female students in Mexican society; and Table 6-4 shows the cosmos of respect according to the statements of female students of American society.

Tables 6-5 and 6-6 chart the transcultural comparison. Since this is the most important aspect of this study, these tables will be described in the following section, in which the results of the transcultural comparison are analyzed and discussed.

Transcultural Comparison

Let us analyze now the statistically significant differences in the transcultural comparison. Table 6-5 shows the comparison of the male Mexican students' attitudes with those of the male American students. An effort has been made to include all data in which significant differences exist between the two cultures. Thus it will be observed that, besides making comparisons within the qualitative categories with which we have familiarized ourselves, we indicate with a plus or minus sign to whom the difference is favorable or detrimental; and immediately following the plus or minus sign is shown the quantitative category to which the datum belongs in each society. Thus we can clearly see, for example, that, even though old men are highly respected in both societies (HR), they receive significantly more respect in Mexico (+) than in the United States (−). It will also be observed that in other cases, like that of young men, who receive medium respect (MR) in Mexico and high respect (HR) in the United States, the statistical difference favors the United States (+) over Mexico (−).

Let us now observe and discuss the results by qualitative categories, beginning with the category of age and sex. I was surprised to find that in the United States young boys, baby boys, young women, teen-age girls, young girls, and baby girls are accorded less respect than in Mexico. From what we know about infantile psychology in the United States we would have expected the opposite, particularly in regard to younger children. Of course our data are conscious sociocultural data, and the good intentions indicated by the male Mexican students perhaps might not extend to their actions. But the impression remains that the problem could be much more complex.

Naturally one must remember that in the United States respect generally means admiring someone considered superior, wishing to treat others on an equal basis, giving opportunities to others, etc., while in Mexico, as Essay 5 shows, to respect generally means to love someone, to feel affection for someone, to give and receive protection, etc.; younger children as well as young women and girls, etc., could only with difficulty elicit respect as it is defined in the United States, but on the contrary they could easily elicit the Mexican type of respect.

But perhaps there may be deeper waters here. Maslow and Díaz-Guerrero say: "The visitor to Mexico soon notices that Mexican children behave differently from American children. The general impression is that the Mexican children are better behaved, more polite, more helpful. . . . Mexican children seem to resent authority less, to demand less, to be less whining and complaining . . . to cry less often. . . . They laugh more and seem to enjoy themselves more."[8]

In the category of the immediate family, older brothers, older sisters, and younger brothers receive more respect in Mexico than in the United States. In both cultures, of course, they all receive high respect, just as all the immediate family does. Among the males of this study, in the category of age and sex, as we have seen, and in other categories as we shall see later, there is *a decided difference in according respect to the extremes of age*, a difference which favors Mexico. There is also an obvious difference, one which is on the whole independent of the criterion of age, although there is a definite tendency to associate it with early ages, *in favor of the female sex* in Mexico. In regard to older people, the difference of the cultures seems to favor the expression of respect for the male sex in Mexico.

In regard to the collateral family, grandfathers, uncles, and aunts, who receive high respect in both cultures, receive differentially greater respect in Mexico than in the United States, and younger

[8] Abraham H. Maslow and R. Díaz-Guerrero, "Delinquency as a Value Disturbance," in *Festschrift for Gardner Murphy*, ed. J. G. Peatman and E. L. Hartley, pp. 228–229.

female cousins receive a definitely higher respect in Mexico than in the United States. Once more we observe slight tendencies favoring the older male and the younger female in the expression of respect in Mexico.

In the category of friends, older friends, who are highly respected in both cultures, receive differentially less respect in Mexico than in the United States. This conflicts with the general interpretative attitude that we have been forming.

In the category of neighbors there are no statistical differences for the population studied.

In the category of occupations, laborers and servants receive high respect in Mexico and only medium respect in the United States. As for ministers, who receive high respect in both cultures, they are significantly more respected in the United States than in Mexico.

The category of economic positions gives us a series of very interesting results. Members of the middle class, who are highly respected in both cultures, receive significantly higher respect in Mexico. As for the members of the lower class and the poor, they are highly respected in Mexico and receive only medium respect in the United States, making the statistical difference between these groups quite significant.

Finally, the wealthy, who receive only medium respect in both cultures, receive significantly more respect in Mexico than in the United States. These differences regarding the relationship between respect and economic position, together with the differences regarding the occupations of laborer and servant—and interestingly also the very marked difference in regard to beggars (which also favors Mexico, where they receive high respect, while they receive little respect in the United States)—are among the most consistent differences found in this particular study. As we shall see later, almost parallel differences are observed between female Mexican students and female American students. It is here perhaps that we find one of the sharpest differences in the social attitudes of the Mexican and the American. We have already stated that frequently in the United States economic position and status can be taken as synonymous. It is precisely here, then, that a great number of fantastic contradictions can come into play and can lead to faulty communication, even for sociologists of both nations. Earlier we indicated that respect can be considered as one of the factors or ingredients that participate in the formation of the status of an individual in a particular society. This being so, people of low socioeconomic status in Mexico can have high status in social respect. This would be clearly contradictory in American society. This tremendous contradiction between the meanings given to the idea of respect in the two nations and in the attribution of respect to individuals belonging to the cultures perhaps finds its clearest expression in the high respect given to beggars by the male Mexican student and the low respect these individuals receive within American society. And we insist on the example of the beggar, because the very idea of the beggar in Mexico often includes the following ingredients: persons who would have nothing within society, who would be a kind of zero in society, if it were not that they received something from this society, at least in terms of respect, etc. At the same time, given the American meaning of respect, respect that is generally won through a demonstration of capability and efficiency or of superiority in some activity, and given an attitude that holds, in effect, that all human beings are equal and have equal opportunities, the stereotype of the beggar is that of the individual who has not taken advantage—as the situation would probably be rationalized—of the opportunities afforded him to achieve equality with others. The beggar, then, is a flagrant contradiction of American ideals.

Finally, among the miscellaneous items, we find that the constitution is highly respected in both countries, but significantly more so in Mexico, and that, on the contrary, "equals" are significantly less respected in Mexico than in the United States. In this last case we see reaffirmed the idea that, in effect, the sociocultural ideals of the American are democratic and stress the equality of human beings. Certain items slightly more remote from daily life, as are the somewhat more philosophic aspects of the constitution, receive greater respect in Mexico than in the United States, perhaps because of the theoretical idealism of the Mexican.

Let us pass quickly now to the transcultural comparison of the female students of Mexico and of the United States (Table 6-6). We find, in the first place, that the difference in regard to young men is the only difference to be maintained of those we encountered among the males in the area of age and sex. From the female students, as from the males, young men receive medium respect in Mexico and high respect in the United States, with a significant difference that differentially favors youth above the extremes of age in the United States.

In regard to the immediate family, the Mexican women are different from American women in that they have greater respect for older brothers.

In the collateral family, we find significant differences that favor the women of the United States in the amount of respect given to younger male and female cousins.

Passing to the category of friends, we find once again that the American woman is definitely more inclined than the Mexican woman to give respect in this area, so that older male friends, younger male friends, and older female friends receive differentially greater respect from the American woman than from the Mexican woman.

In the category of neighbors, again the American women show greater respect for older and younger female neighbors than do the Mexican women.

In the area of occupations the differences are multiple and in almost all cases favor the American woman; even though the Mexican woman gives high respect to the majority of the following occupations, the American woman gives them significantly greater respect. The occupations referred to are those of priest, minister, lawyer, engineer, artist, doctor, and intellectual. On the other hand, there are clear differences in the level of respect that laborers and servants receive, and these differences favor the Mexican woman.

When we turn to economic position we find differences very similar to those we have already indicated for the men. In this case, the Mexican woman gives significantly more respect than the American woman to members of the lower class, to the poor, to the wealthy, and to beggars.

Finally, among the miscellaneous items, the American woman

Table 6-6
Transcultural Comparison
Female Preparatory Students in Mexico and Female Undergraduates in the United States

	Mexico + or − R	Mexico Q.C.	United States + or − R	United States Q.C.
Age and sex				
Young men	−	MR	+	HR
Friends				
Older male friends	−	HR	+	HR
Younger male friends	−	LR	+	MR
Older female friends	−	HR	+	HR
Immediate family				
Older brothers	+	HR	−	HR
Neighbors				
Older female neighbors	−	HR	+	HR
Younger female neighbors	−	LR	+	MR
Collateral family				
Younger male cousins	−	MR	+	MR
Younger female cousins	−	MR	+	MR
Occupations				
Priests	−	HR	+	HR
Ministers	−	MR	+	HR
Lawyers	−	HR	+	HR
Engineers	−	HR	+	HR
Artists	−	MR	+	HR
Doctors	−	HR	+	HR
Intellectuals	−	HR	+	HR
Laborers	+	HR	−	MR
Servants	+	MR	−	MR
Miscellaneous items				
Equals	−	MR	+	HR
Classmates	−	HR	+	HR
Economic position				
Low-class people	+	HR	−	LR
Poor people	+ + +	HR	−	MR
Wealthy people	+ +	MR	−	LR
Beggars	+ +	HR	−	LR

+ or − R: more or less respect in the given culture, as compared to the other culture
Q.C.: quantitative category of respect
HR: high respect
MR: medium respect
LR: little respect
The cultural differences shown are statistically significant by proof of Chi square and to a level of 0.05 or more.

gives significantly more respect to her equals and classmates than does the Mexican woman.

It has probably escaped no one, and this is one of the most clear-cut results of this study, that the male Mexican preparatory-school student is definitely more active in selecting who ought to receive respect than is the American male student. And it is no less striking to realize that, among the female students, it is the Americans who seem to establish actively the greater number of areas in which respect is due. Later intracultural analyses, which will compare the man and the woman of the Mexican culture to each other, and the man and the woman of American culture to each other, will show us exactly where the difference lies. A first review of the data seems to indicate, nonetheless, that the great difference occurs between the extremely active attitude of the Mexican male in selecting the members of his society who should receive respect and the very passive attitude of the Mexican woman in this respect; while in American society the man and the woman appear to be equally active, if very possibly in a manner that differentiates among the areas where respect should be rendered. In any case, and in regard to the present transcultural comparison of Mexican and American women, we observe that their differences in relation to the characteristics of age and sex and of immediate family are quite small, and that the area of great activity (and a very superior activity on the part of the American woman) concerns some minor aspects of the collateral family, and especially the aspects involving socializing with individuals outside the family, such as friends in general, female neighbors, male neighbors, and, in particular, significant figures from religion and the professions. This difference in favor of the American woman shows us the high level of socializing that she has achieved compared to the Mexican woman, who, interested fundamentally (although not more absolutely than the American) in her immediate family and in those closest to her, seems to act at a distance from all other individuals outside the family, such as friends, neighbors, and religious and professional figures. This is an interesting difference that this study has captured in the attribution of respect in both cultures.

In succinct form we can say, then, first, that this study has attempted to clarify the differences in the attribution of respect in American society and in Mexican society. Second, this differentiation has been based on data obtained through a questionnaire given to Mexican preparatory-school students and American undergraduates. Third, this work has demonstrated beyond all doubt that there are a great number of differences in the attribution of respect in the two cultures, among both men and women. Fourth, it should be noted that the differences among male students show us that the Mexican male allots differentially greater respect to the extremes of chronological age, with a certain tendency to consider older males and younger females with greater respect, and, in general terms, also show that the feminine sex receives much greater respect from the Mexican male than from the American male. Turning to the relation of economic position and occupation to respect, we find a definite tendency in favor of the Mexican male to respect people of all social classes; the difference is particularly clear in the respect accorded to members of the lower class, poor people, and beggars, as well as to occupations low on the economic scale, such as those of laborer and servant. In addition, the wealthy seem to receive, in what might seem a contradiction at first but in reality is not, greater respect in Mexico than in the United States. On the other hand, the difference favors the United States in the allotment of respect to young men and to equals and, somewhat unexpectedly, to older male friends.

Fifth, among the female students we observe an interesting superiority in allotting respect on the part of the American woman, and this superiority seems to be based fundamentally on the greater socializing of the American woman, who is equal to the Mexican woman in allotting respect to her immediate family, etc., but who also allots respect to people more distant from the family group, such as friends, neighbors, professional figures, and religious leaders. In contrast, the Mexican woman seems to show differentially greater respect for the lower class, the poor, and beggars, as well as for laborers and servants, than the American woman; it can be seen that this attribution of respect in relation to economic position presents the same difference found among the men.

Sixth, the respect we have been studying seems to be attributed in

American society on the basis of what individuals perform or produce, and in Mexican culture it seems to be attributed according to the dictates of the culture itself.

Comments by R. Díaz-Guerrero

In other works, I refer to what I have been calling *sociocultural premises*.[9] I believe that these premises are the mainspring, hidden in the web of personality, that determines verbal behavior and often also determines the actions that have moved various authors to speak of a national character. On this occasion, I wish to hypothesize the existence of at least two sociocultural premises or presuppositions in the Mexican that, in my opinion, might clarify his type of respect.

The first premise would be that " 'Human' values are more important than economic values in regard to respect." Then, if the American premise were the opposite, I would permit myself to hypothesize that one of the grave difficulties faced by Americans in making friends internationally would result from that premise. Not only that, but, if such a premise should exist, semiconsciously or even unconsciously, in the American socioculture, it would not surprise me in the least that the problem of racial discrimination should be tied in with that premise. Nevertheless, we do not believe that it can simply be said that the American sociocultural presupposition is that "Economic values are more important than human values"; we must add, since it has been demonstrated by the two studies carried out by Dr. Peck and the writer of this paper, that a profound American sociocultural premise could be that "All human beings are born equal; they have equal opportunities; and therefore we shall respect only those who take advantage of these opportunities to become economically strong." The sad part is that this beautiful idealism of equality could be at least the partial culprit in leading to or provoking such sociocultural premises or presuppositions as "Economic val-

[9] R. Díaz-Guerrero, "Symposium on Culture and Child Development," *American Journal of Orthopsychiatry* 31, no. 3 (1961): 518–520; idem, "Differences in Mexican and U.S. National Character and Their Implications for Public Health Practice"; idem, *Hacia una teoría histórico-bio-psico-socio-cultural del comportamiento humano.*

ues are more important than human values," and to an external
sociocultural *appearance* that seems to justify the application of
nicknames like "dollar imperialists" to the Americans. Thus it would
be constantly necessary to counterbalance the ideals of equality with
humanitarian ideals, which have always implied a considerable
amount of protection or paternalism, not only on the "social" level,
but also on the level of *individual human being to individual human
being.* In regard to this, it is to be hoped that Mexicans will finally
develop a democracy in which equality increases parallel to their
highly valuable sense of respect through love and of reciprocal protection among human beings. Our studies show that some of the
basic material for such a democracy already exists in the Mexican
socioculture, at least in the form that the student visualizes it, but, of
course, it is still to be realized. This realization, naturally, has met and
will continue to meet with multiple and extraordinarily difficult obstacles, obstacles of external reality and, especially, obstacles implicit in the nature of the human being and in the nature of human
relations. It is to be hoped that one day we Mexicans will manage to
overcome them.

A second premise—in this case, perhaps more than a premise: a
sociocultural presupposition of the Mexican—will allow us to round
out our understanding of the Mexican's unique form of generously
allotting respect. We speak of "presupposition" because we believe
that in this case the Mexican, in general, would not be able to express
the concept coherently; that is, he acts according to a semiconscious
or perhaps in some cases totally unconscious Mexican sociocultural
premise; for example, "The choice of who should receive more or less
respect and who should not in their roles or social attributes is predetermined by beliefs, traditions, etc., much more than by the individual merits of the individuals." The old man receives respect because he *is* old ("The devil knows more because he's old than because
he's a devil"), the woman because she *is* a woman, the boy and the
girl because they *are* a boy and a girl, the beggar because he *is* a beggar, and not for their worthy qualities or their achievements, which in
the last case must be almost nil. The corresponding American premise, clear and conscious, would stipulate the following: "Respect

will be given to those persons who earn it for their worthy qualities or their achievements, without regard to age, sex, etc., and respect will not be given to those who have not made themselves deserving of it." Here we have a demand that justice be rendered absolutely, free from the beliefs or traditions or formulas of traditional societies. In this case, we believe, the American socioculture has taken an important and progressive step toward realizing those ideals that children and youths in general develop: a real and objective justice in regard to who ought to receive the prestige and other advantages of being respected and who should not. Like children and youths, however, Americans seem to base their ideals on the idea of man's perfection or, at least, on the idea that all human beings are "full of life, of enthusiasm, and inexhaustible energy," or that "Nothing is easier than to tell good from bad." In their enthusiasm they seem to forget that life is far from having such perfection and elegant simplicity in all its human reaches. If they would learn from the painful experience of old cultures, they would know that the human being is very far from perfect, and that, before establishing something similar to that justice which seems quite utopian at present, man must be freed from at least some of his great shackles: emotional immaturity, anguish, pessimism, illness, etc.

In any case, it is our opinion that, in their experimental development of ways of conceiving human relationships, the two cultures have established different premises, and we believe that we have convinced the reader that the premises we have stipulated for both groups, if nothing more, clarify the differences demonstrated in their attribution of respect.

7. Sociocultural Premises, Attitudes, and Cross-Cultural Research

Introduction

"Men are superior to women." From observation of the behavior of men vis-à-vis women in Mexico, we derived the belief that such a statement might be a valid sociocultural premise (SCP)[1] for most of the Mexican people. Thus, when it came to a description of the Mexican family structure, further observation permitted us to say, "The Mexican family is founded upon two fundamental propositions: (1) the unquestioned and absolute supremacy of the father; and (2) the necessary and absolute self-sacrifice of the mother."[2] From these two generalized SCPs we were able to organize a fairly complete and accurate description of what goes on in the Mexican family. At the time we did not doubt that this constellation was a logical conclusion

NOTE. Reprinted from the *International Journal of Psychology*, 1967, vol. 2, pp. 79–87, by permission of the International Union of Psychological Science and Dunod Editeur, Paris.

[1] A broader, more comprehensive term might be *historico-sociocultural* premise.

[2] Essay 1.

drawn from the two main statements. Indeed, it all hung together, but there were also several unrealized, and even now difficult to verbalize, links in the pattern. What follows is an attempt to verbalize such links.

First and foremost, such premises apparently provoke what we may call an "automatic evaluation" of the premises and the roles governed by the premises. Thus, from the necessary and absolute self-sacrifice of the mother there emerges at least one other SCP, which is held with greater strength than its "originator." It is that "The mother is the dearest person in existence."[3]

From what we may call the *meaning atmosphere* created by this maternal abnegation and by this profound affect toward the mother, there emerge attitudinal mental tendencies that, inferred and verbalized as SCPs, could take the forms: "The maternal role has a high prestige value"; "The mother is an extremely important figure"; "A mother has a high social status in Mexico" (independent of socioeconomic position);[4] "Mothers are highly respected." The atmosphere created by this tight constellation of major SCPs provides for the appearance of a number of minor SCPs, such as: "A child should obey his mother"; "A child should honor his mother"; "A child should respect his mother"; "A child owes respect, obedience, and love to his mother"; "One should never disobey his mother." We have wondered a great deal about the mental mechanism that intervenes between these meaning atmospheres that we have verbalized as a major group of SCPs and each of the minor SCPs. Man has singled out, quite brilliantly, a clearly recognizable portion of these mechanisms ever since Aristotle. It is logic. Often, particularly when a socioculture verbalizes an SCP clearly and consciously, its syllogistic logical conclusions become SCPs too. Thus, Mexicans have clearly verbalized that "The authority of the father is absolute and unquestionable," and subjects of both sexes adhere overwhelmingly to the statements "A father's word should never be questioned" and "A son (or a daugh-

[3] Essay 4; R. Díaz-Guerrero, "Una escala factorial de premisas histórico-socioculturales de la familia mexicana," *Interamerican Journal of Psychology* 6, nos. 3–4 (1972): 235–244.

[4] See Essay 6.

ter) should never question orders from the father."[5] But the statement "A mother's word should never be questioned" brings similarly overwhelming support, and in this case the pure logical mechanism is not so clear.

The data for these statements come from two studies.[6] In the first, the figures were arrived at from the tabulated results of 294 returned questionnaires. The questionnaires were distributed in Mexico City following Malcolm Cantril's weighted random-sample technique. Cooperation was 57%. Only adults over eighteen years old were represented. The second study was carried out using Richard D. Trent's extension and stabilization of the original Díaz-Guerrero questionnaire.[7] It was applied to 472 high-school students from seventeen high schools in the City of Mexico selected to represent different areas of the City and different socioeconomic levels. Seven schools were all male, six were for mixed sexes, and four were all female. In the Díaz-Guerrero questionnaire, statements were presented and could be answered by "yes," "no," and "I don't know." In the Trent-Díaz-Guerrero questionnaire the subject would place a check before those statements that he agreed with. Table 7-1 is self-explanatory.

The statement "A mother's word should never be questioned" is perhaps reached after much action from a constellation of SCPs that are "consonant" or "congruous" with it. I have been fascinated by the way in which small children regularize all verbs. The result is just as if they had clearly verbalized the following: "All verbs are regular (their endings follow a rule); I think is a verb; therefore: I thinked." Here we have an early and clear case of the many similar phenomena that seem to arise from the formation of a meaning atmosphere. The results that emerge uncannily resemble the syllogistic logical mechanism. At any rate, the mechanisms of action for the SCPs within the human mind appear to be "automatic evaluations," and one is reminded of Charles E. Osgood's semantic differential. Meaning atmos-

[5] Díaz-Guerrero, "Una escala factorial."

[6] See Essay 4 and Díaz-Guerrero, "Una escala factorial."

[7] E. D. Maldonado Sierra, Richard D. Trent, and R. Fernández Marina, "Three Basic Themes in Mexican and Puerto Rican Family Values," *Journal of Social Psychology* 48 (1958): 167–181.

Table 7-1
Percentages of Agreement with Statements

	First Study		Second Study			
	M (%)	F (%)	M (%)	MM (%)	FM (%)	F (%)
The mother is the dearest person in existence.	95	86	90	90	95	88
A father's word should never be questioned.			84	72	75	74
A son should never question orders from his father.			70	68	66	66
A daughter should never question orders from her father.			69	69	66	65
A mother's word should never be questioned.			83	76	88	82

M: males; in the second study, students at all-male secondary schools
F: females; in the second study, students at all-female secondary schools
MM: male students at mixed secondary schools
FM: female students at mixed secondary schools

pheres and Leon Festinger's dissonance and Osgood's congruity also come to mind, as well as syllogistic logic.

Socioculture and Sociocultural Premises

For the purposes of this paper, let us perceive a socioculture as a system of interrelated sociocultural premises that govern or provide norms for feelings, ideas, the hierarchization of interpersonal relations, the stipulation of the types of roles to be fulfilled, and the rules for the interaction of individuals in such roles: where, when, with whom, and how to play them. All of this is valid for interactions within the family, the collateral family, the groups, the society, and the institutional superstructures (educational, religious, governmental), and for such problems as the main goals of life, the way of facing life, the perception of humanity, the problems of sex, masculinity and femininity, the economy, death, etc.

What is a sociocultural premise? An SCP is an affirmation, simple or complex, that seems to provide the basis for the specific logic of the group. We say that, when the members of a given group think, their thinking starts from these affirmations properly called premises; when they feel, their way of feeling can be predicated from these premises. When they act, they will implement these premises or their conclusions unless, as we shall see later, a more powerful inner or outer force interferes.

Regarding their genesis for a given generation, we believe that these affirmations are learned as such, *as affirmations*, from the significant and authorized figures in the sociocultural context. These figures are predominantly the parents, but the SCPs are usually reinforced by almost every other adult in the sociocultural group, by older brothers and sisters, and often by institutions—social, educational, religious, governmental, etc. We have already stated that they are also engendered from the meaning atmospheres enacted by several previously learned SCPs, or they are acquired through automatic evaluation of other SCPs.

Let us enumerate the social functions of the SCPs. They equip individuals for easier interpersonal, group, society, and international communication. They are, therefore, a *sine qua non* for social living. They are the basis for understandable communication among humans, who otherwise would have a total confusion of individual languages. They are the essential units of interpersonal reality, that is, the essential units of human reality understandable to the group, and usually fully understandable only to the given group. They make up the most important basis for the creation of the interpersonal and group reality that we have, in another paper, contrasted with the physical reality.[8] We are even suggesting that they are the basis for the only form of communication that is meaningful to most people in the world. We are suggesting that there is almost no human communication unless there is an agreement beforehand about what is communicated or about the premises from which it derives. In other words, almost all so-called human communication is sociocultural. We might even infer from these statements that one of the great difficulties for international communication is the lack of existence of

[8] See Essay 2.

SCPs that are valid to all human groups. Which are the world-wide SCPs? On one side the statement of the Rights of Man, on the other the Third International. Thus far they have proven pitifully inadequate as powerful universal SCPs or even as a basis for lore and folklore.

It has been stated previously that the SCPs will provide norms for the thinking of the individuals of a given group. This, of course, refers to the so-called normal population. As a matter of fact what makes it "normal" is its spontaneous or easy allegiance to the SCPs of the group. In these circumstances we would expect that the SCPs would predict, at least, the written answers of an anonymous or cooperative subject answering a questionnaire about them. We shall consider this one of the operational baselines to demonstrate the presence or action of a given SCP. We shall call this the questionnaire threshold or, generally, the written-test threshold. We can determine another reference point: actual behavior. We shall call this the behavioral threshold. With these baselines determined, we can theorize about the factors that will facilitate and the factors that will interfere with the action of the SCPs.

What are the facilitating factors? (a) The SCPs and their conclusions will move in their action first toward the questionnaire threshold and then toward the behavioral threshold, the more the interpersonal or group environment is in agreement with them. Thus, for example, the SCPs and their conclusions will be commanding behavior at the family level, immediate-group level, provincial level, and national level for the given socioculture more than they would be in the presence of other sociocultural groups or at a cosmopolitan level. We have proven, at the questionnaire threshold, statistically significant reductions of strength of male and female SCPs in mixed high schools of Mexico City.[9] (b) The strength of the SCPs will increase when in addition the group provides the emotional tone and the fluid environment for which the SCPs were made, that is, if the anticipations for their expression in the outside world are met. (c) SCPs will probably gain strength too if their predicted behavior leads to gain—in eco-

9 Díaz-Guerrero, "Una escala factorial."

nomic terms, in status, in prestige—and if they lead to immediate or delayed reduction of personal and interpersonal stress. (d) Strength will increase also whenever the group or the society lends them strong backing, publicizes them, and whenever the members of the group or society are willing to endure high stress before giving them up.

Let us now enumerate the hindering factors. (a) Genetic deficiencies and acquired organic pathology may interfere with the learning and development of the SCPs. (b) Interference may also be found at the psychological level because of personal inability to accept the SCPs or because of rebellion against them. Here we have, fundamentally, the action of the psychodynamic factors. Psychodynamic mechanisms, defenses, and neuroses can best be seen as acting at the personal level, as individual rebellions against the SCPs. Incidentally, Freudian psychoanalysis was conceived as a rebellion against some of the SCPs of the Victorian Era. (c) We may perceive the genetic, physiological, and psychodynamic factors as provoking reduction in the strength of the SCPs. The measure of their effect can be obtained, either at the questionnaire or at the behavioral threshold. (d) The strength of the SCPs will decrease if bringing them into action will lead to interpersonal stress. (e) One might like to generalize and say that the SCPs' strength will be diminished as a function of the amount of stress—biological, psychodynamic, or interpersonal—that must be faced to bring them up to the questionnaire or the behavioral threshold. (f) The SCPs will diminish in strength with the decline of backing from the group, with the disorganization of the group, and with the formation of subgroups. (g) Individualism, if brought to bear upon these patterns of thinking, will tend to diminish their strength. (h) Cynicism about the lack of meaningfulness of the SCPs for the individual world may effectively diminish the strength of the SCPs. Cynicism will not function, however, if the subjects are fully aware that the role of the SCPs is to facilitate interpersonal and intergroup interaction rather than individual satisfaction. (i) Dissonance experiments have proven their effect on attitudes.[10] It is felt

[10] I refer here to the dissonance experiments of Dr. Leon Festinger. A simple introduction to this series of experiments can be found in *Scientific American*.

that they will have an effect on SCPs only if their public disavowal is made in front of a sympathetic group and not if the listening public disapproves.

If we look into the literature we find that the term *attitudes* is used to refer to many forms of readiness to feel, think, or act in a somewhat predetermined way. We might even say that the SCPs are nothing but group attitudes, but little would be gained. The main impression obtained is that attitudes are identified with the actual written expression of a view toward an event, an issue, etc. Actually, social psychologists have studied specific attitudes, right and left, and only recently have related them to more generalized attitudes. Not much has been done, however, to study the nature of attitude, its connection with other mental processes, or the mechanism by which it carries on its action within the mind. Investigators have frequently looked at attitudes from the point of view of their relationship to behavior. Partially because of this, they have been found to be based on many factors. On the contrary we have seen that the SCPs are more permanent. Also they are a priori, supraindividual, group determinants of thinking, feeling, and action—and, clearly, a group language.

To relate SCPs to prevalent learning theories may be more difficult in some respects than in others. We have seen how some SCPs come into existence out of automatic evaluations and how others appear to come into existence as conclusions from meaning atmospheres. Finally, others owe their existence to the patterns of syllogistic logic. We may assume, if these SCPs obtained from various sources are functional, that they have been learned. It appears difficult to relate such emergences to the usual mechanisms of the learning theories. In other respects, however, particularly in regard to the factors that we have enumerated for the reduction or the increase of strength of the SCPs, the learning theories may be variously helpful. We have seen the same to be true for psychodynamic or psychoanalytic variables.

The Active-Passive Dichotomy

It is relatively simple to infer SCPs about the family and the roles of the sexes. The knowledge that they affect the thinking, feeling, and behavior of the Mexicans indicates their importance for that area of cross-cultural research.[11] Modern research on attitudes, however, has gone further, at least in the United States and a few other places, to the search for basic, all-important attitudinal dimensions or structural principles of mental functioning that may explain more of the variability of common attitudes. Cross-culturally, we need to ascertain SCPs of world-wide value, to classify cultures according to them, and to find, within each culture, their relation to the local SCPs. Somewhat accidentally, we may have fallen upon one such SCP.

I was breaking my head trying to figure out why Americans are so active and make efficiency so much the point of departure in the evaluation of people, and why Mexicans are traditionally considered lazy, are not concerned with efficiency, and make their evaluations of people predominantly from how much interpersonal fun they derive from them. McClelland's finding that individuals with a high need achievement made a harder criticism of their parents than other individuals appeared relevant.[12] Even more relevant is E. G. French's study.[13] She found that subjects with high need achievement and low affiliation motivation chose for a working partner a competent nonfriend. Those with high affiliation and low need achievement chose a friend even if less competent. That explanation was temporarily satisfying. At the time the concern was akin to the relationship of affiliation to efficiency in the two cultures. The apparent need for activity of the ones and the apparent need for idleness of the others kept bothering me. American sayings came to mind: "An idle mind is a devil's workshop"; "Work never hurt anybody; it's worrying about it that gets you down"; "Hard work is the best for you"; "There is no rest for the wicked, and the good are always busy"; "Fool away time." In Mexico similar sayings have all been distorted, and we have: "Do not today what you can do tomorrow"; "Idleness is the mother of a delightful life [es la madre de una vida padre]"; "Work brutalizes [el trabajo embrutece]"; "Work is sacred; don't touch it."

[11] See Essay 4 and Díaz-Guerrero, "Una escala factorial."
[12] David C. McClelland et al., The Achievement Motive.
[13] E. G. French, "Motivation as a Variable in Work-Partner Selection," Journal of Abnormal and Social Psychology 53 (1956): 96–99.

Suddenly all became clear: Mexicans wanted to avoid stress, and Americans wanted to face it. The two cultures somehow had come to decide how life should be lived, and Americans had decided: "Let us face stress," while Mexicans decided: "Let us try and avoid it." These, we felt, were the generalized SCPs behind the open attitudes. Months later we were forced to realize that Mexicans undergo as much stress as do Americans, if not more. Why, of course, nobody can avoid stress! What happens is that Mexicans face it passively while Americans face it actively. Mexicans, we said then, are passive endurers of stress and Americans are active endurers of stress. Suddenly, I, a Mexican, and my Australian-American wife could understand many single incidents of total misunderstanding between Mexicans and Americans, the most common being the scandalized "Why don't they do something about it?" in the presence of too many ill-fed children, poverty, dirt, or sickness of Mexicans. But their virtue is that they can, where the Americans could not, passively endure all such misery. It was as if the Mexicans held as an SCP the following: "Life is a tough proposition, and the best way to deal with it is to passively endure what it brings." Soon I realized that such an approach to life in Mexico is solidly backed. It is virtuous; abnegation, obedience, self-sacrifice, submission, dependence, politeness, courtesy—all forms of passive endurance—are Mexican sociocultural virtues. The prevalent religion and the pre-Cortesian agreed that "this is a valley of tears." The prevalent easy adjustment of the Mexican to tragedy, even death; the *ni modo* ("what can anyone do, there is no way"); the widespread use of proverbs, stories, and jokes of a quasi-stoic philosophy; the strong fatalistic attitudes—all these are beautiful examples of a well-integrated and well-learned philosophy indicating that the very best way, indeed, the righteous way to endure stress is passively. I do not have to say that the prevalent American philosophy makes a virtue of the active endurance of stress and considers it the best possible way "to face reality." Life is lived best in constant activity. This is the solution to the problem of life, and even the travel agencies know about this. Keep them hopping, having fun. Self-esteem decays if you are idle. Remember the studies of Paul Lazarsfeld and P. Eisenberg.[14]

[14] Paul Lazarsfeld, "An Unemployed Village," *Character and Personality* 1

It is felt that, since dealing or coping with the stress of life is a universal phenomenon, sociocultures can be conveniently classified as active or passive endurers of stress dichotomy. To classify sociocultures thus will immediately identify a large number of important correlates, and field observations or tests will easily verify such correlates. Since the business of how to live life, that is, how best to endure its stress, is the business of every human being, cross-cultural research in this area will be seen with interest everywhere. Since whether one belongs to a passive-endurer or to an active-endurer socioculture has tremendously important implications for economic development, social change, etc., its study should be preferential. Since it is predicted that "underdeveloped" nations will have passive-endurer-of-stress sociocultures, the study of this problem is indispensable for contemporary decisions.

Let us see, then, the breadth of the application of this dichotomy by hypothetically predicting findings in different fields. It should be possible to demonstrate by the proper measurements in biology, physiology, psychodynamics, social psychology, sociology, etc., that active endurers of stress (AES) have a low endurance of passive stress and passive endurers of stress (PES) have a low endurance of active stress. R. S. Lazarus and his associates have found that achievement-motivated and affiliation-motivated people will have differently high arousal of stress when exposed to inability to satisfy their specific needs.[15] We are suggesting, for the AES-PES dichotomy, that people endure the familiar stresses more effectively and longer.

Psychologically, the AES should value conflict, competition, action, aggressiveness, equality, individual freedom, opportunity, independence, informality, content rather than form, and pragmatism. They should feel guilt for the use of energy "just for fun." PES should value harmony, protection, dependence, cooperation, idleness, prescribed roles, formality, form rather than content, and platonic philosophy.

(1932): 147–151; P. Eisenberg and Paul Lazarsfeld, "The Psychological Effects of Unemployment," *Psychological Bulletin* 35 (1938): 358–390.

[15] R. S. Lazarus, "A Program of Research in Psychological Stress," in *Festschrift for Gardner Murphy*, ed. J. G. Peatman and E. L. Hartley, pp. 313–329.

Psychodynamically, for the same amount of frustration the PES will produce less aggression. Psychosomatically, more hypertension, stomach ulcers, and coronaries should occur in active endurers.[16]

Psychiatrically there should be more hypochondriasis, neurasthenia, and hysteria in passive endurers. Socially, there should be more racial intolerance and discrimination in active endurers; more intolerance also for social deviants, mental illness (Osgood found that in the United States neurotics are seen as bad, weak, and inactive), physical illness, alcoholism; and, in passive endurers, more economic exploitation; greater economic distance between the rich and the poor, the rich and the middle class; greater personal, emotional, and economic exploitation of one individual by another.

Criminologically, in AES there should be more crime for economic gain and in PES more crime as the result of reaching the limits of passive endurance in emotional problems. Demographically, a larger size of family and overpopulation can be expected in PES. Active endurers of stress will more often try to convert others to their views than PES. PES will agree with others, enduring their actual disagreement to avoid active interpersonal stress. In religion, Catholicism is mainly a PES philosophy and Protestantism an AES philosophy.

Socioeconomically, change—and, if possible, rapid change—is good and virtuous and right for AES, and it is not right, virtuous, or particularly good for the others. It may be seen with some degree of suspicion and at the very least with reservations. Economic philosophies can also be classified: capitalism and Marxism-Leninism are both AES philosophies. The second is, however, a far more extreme reaction to PES, more often leading to violence (the struggle of the classes), and, in practice, ending in a greater imposition of stress on individuals, who still, characteristically, endure it passively.

[16] The word *stress* has been used here mainly in the way that Hans Selye understands it in *The Stress of Life*. However, there is difficulty in relating the concept of passive and active endurance of stress to Selye's triphasic scheme of stress. It must be realized that his experiments with animals were carried out under forced passive-endurance-of-stress conditions. When he relates the alarm reaction to psychosomatic illness, he differentiates between syndromes resulting from insufficient and from excessive alarm reactions. Hesitantly, we would relate passive endurance to insufficient alarm and active endurance to excessive alarm.

At the national and international level, pacifist, neutral, and non-interventionist nations should have mostly passive-endurance-of-stress sociocultures, and the contrary is true for the leaders of the two contemporary blocks. AES nations will go to war more often and more easily than PES nations. The Germany of the past (and perhaps the Germany of today) is one extreme example of an AES sociocul-ture. (Other variables, like the effects of authority in the learning of sociocultural patterns, must be brought in to understand differences between, for instance, the German AES and North American AES.) AES nations will more often try to convince other nations of their political and socioeconomic views.

AES nations will more easily discriminate racially, economically, and socially than PES nations. The high anticipation of AES and their relative inability to passively endure stress predispose them to discrimination. Recent literature on prejudice finds positive correla-tions between social mobility (a form of active endurance of stress) and degree of prejudice.[17] Socioculturally, one would expect a far greater number of majority-shared SCPs and more organic SCP sys-tems in PES societies than in AES societies. One would expect obe-dience and authority to be far more important in PES societies. The greater the desire to avoid AES, the greater the number of a priori norms for interaction. Finally, Cervantes's *Don Quijote* was a warn-ing to the Spaniards of what will happen to any PES who suddenly dares to actively endure stress. He simply will end up with far more stress to endure passively. This is Cervantes's own life.

This long and intricate list of meaningful correlates of our inferen-tial and generalized SCPs ("Life has to be lived, and the best way to live it is by actively enduring its stresses" and "Life has to be lived, and the best way to live it is by passively enduring its stresses") may have convinced you of their importance for cross-cultural research. By now it should be fully realized that often these SCPs are nothing more than inferential, inclusive statements that can be translated into any other psychological language—can become, for instance, the theoretical basis for a typology with subdivisions; that is, AES can be

[17] Bruno Bettelheim and M. B. Janowitz, *The Dynamics of Prejudice*.

so because (a) they enjoy active endurance, (b) they consider it good or valuable or virtuous or righteous, (c) they are attracted to it because of need achievement or need for power, (d) they are made in such a way that they cannot act any other way; they cannot endure stress passively. PES can be so because they enjoy passive endurance, because they consider it good, valuable, virtuous, or righteous, or because they cannot act in any other way; they cannot stand active stress. There may of course be pure types and intermediate types; there can also be people who are AES for certain of the stresses of life and PES for certain others, but it is our impression that, outside mental pathology, there will be individual and group consistency in the patterns of dealing with stress.

Summary

An active effort to deal with the problem of stress has been made in this work, in order to present three avenues of approach to the comprehension of what we have called sociocultural premises and their application to cross-cultural research. In the first section, examples drawn from previous research are presented in order to define, perhaps not wholly satisfactorily, what seem to be the fundamental mechanisms of the premises' function within the human mind. Within the range of normality, automatic evaluations of sociocultural premises, classical logic, and the conclusions derived from the meaning atmospheres seem to be the means of their activity.

In the second section, an effort is made to characterize sociocultural premises even further: they are defined as simple or complex affirmations. Human beings may be able to verbalize them clearly, but they may also be totally incapable of verbalizing them, or even of realizing that they exist. In a given group, nevertheless, thought, feeling, and action occur precisely as though the individuals were deriving logical conclusions from these premises. They are learned *as affirmations* made by the significant members of society; they are also derived from meaning atmospheres generated by various previously learned affirmations; and they can be obtained through automatic evaluations of other sociocultural premises. In this section the premises' social function, as well as the sources of their importance and of their strength, is schematized. Operative definitions are sought in relation to the strength of sociocultural premises. Facilitating and hindering factors are enumerated, and certain predictions are made about the fate of sociocultural premises in accordance with these factors. This section ends with a consideration of the relationship of sociocultural premises to the concept of attitudes, and a reconsideration of their relationship to other variables, such as those contained in the theories of learning and of psychoanalysis.

In the third section, we return to examples; examples are given for future research. The importance of sociocultural premises for cross-cultural research is illustrated. Reference is made to recent viewpoints concerning the psychology of attitudes. The urgent need for determining sociocultural premises with world-wide application for cross-cultural research is particularly emphasized. The discovery of one sociocultural premise that possibly fulfills the above-mentioned criteria is described. Immediately afterward follow reasons supporting the validity and importance of this sociocultural premise; a long list of hypotheses to be proven cross-culturally is presented to illustrate the relevance of this premise to widely distributed phenomena, from physiology to culture, and even to international events. Finally, and briefly, related sociocultural premises are mentioned, and a possible typology is selected as an example.

8. The Passive-Active Transcultural Dichotomy

Because of their consistent presence and strength in the answers to several questionnaires, we have become concerned in the past few years with what we call sociocultural premises and their importance in many areas of psychological and psychiatric research. Sociocultural premises, or SCPs, are merely statements used and consistently approved of by most members of a given socioculture. What makes them interesting is that often the thinking and, under certain specified conditions, the behavior of the people who hold to these sociocultural premises are ruled by them or by their conclusions and even by their meaningful extensions. From the knowledge of several "minor" SCPs of a given group, one can sometimes infer the presence of "major" SCPs that may be semiconscious or even unconscious in the given group and yet still exert a strong effect upon a number of areas of behavior. These major, all-embracing SCPs are apparently discovered only when a number of other SCPs for a given group are

Note. This essay originally appeared in the *International Mental Health Research Newsletter* 7, no. 3 (Fall 1965): 8–10, published by the Postgraduate Center for Mental Health, New York.

well known. They, therefore, become easier to ascertain when there are sufficient minor and conscious SCPs from which to infer to the major ones. At the Seventeenth International Congress held in Washington, D.C. in August, 1963, I presented a paper[1] clarifying through a number of examples (a) the specific mechanism by which the SCPs exert their action within the human mind; (b) the functions they fulfill in human behavior; (c) their genesis; (d) the operational base lines needed to demonstrate the presence and the action of given SCPs; (e) the facilitating and hindering factors for their development and activity; and (f) the further characterization of this construct by comparing SCPs with attitudes and by relating SCPs to other variables, such as those developed by learning theories and psychodynamic approaches.

In the last section of the paper, an example was given of an SCP that is inferentially derived and of a high order, which encompasses a large variety of human behavior and appears to be particularly suitable for use in transcultural research.

Assumptions

Beyond the consideration of a number of minor SCPs that permitted the inference, the most important general assumption behind the development of this generalized inclusive SCP is that, in spite of deceptive appearances, such as those implied in the visions of a South Sea island paradise, all humans and all cultures have to deal with a multitude of life stresses.[2] Another general assumption, dealing in this case with the pragmatic value of developing an inferential SCP in this area, is that, in all cultures, men are interested basically

---

[1] Essay 7 in this volume.

[2] The word *stress* is used here almost entirely according to the operational definition given by Hans Selye in *The Stress of Life*. A complete understanding of this concept, in both its biological and its psychological aspects, can be obtained only through studying the works of this author and of others who have subsequently investigated this empirical construct. Nevertheless, we can indicate as possible translations of this concept "the wear and tear involved in confronting the problems of life" and even "the wear and tear involved in the simple act of living." The connotation of *stress* implies a constant biophysical crisis, through which the human being passes as part of the simple act of living and which, naturally, is intensified at times of emergency, constraint, and oppression.

in the problem of how best to deal with stress. A third assumption has to do with the fact that—precisely because stress is such an overriding occurrence in the life of human beings and because they are so interested in finding ways of dealing with it—in their development all cultures have finally arrived at what they consider workable fashions or ways of dealing with life stresses.

After having gone into a number of semi–blind alleys, we finally arrived at the conclusion that, in the main, cultures have arrived—notwithstanding a number of minor deviations from the major trends—at one of the two following conclusions: (a) that the best way to deal with the stresses of life is by facing them actively, or (b) that the best way of dealing with life stresses is by enduring them passively.

Data from Two Cultures

Because of experience and of some collected data, American and Mexican cultures were selected as representatives of these dichotomous ways of dealing with stress. It was pointed out that, for the Mexican, to endure stress passively is not only the best but the most virtuous way. Abnegation in the mother, obedience in the children, self-sacrifice in all, submission, dependence, politeness, courtesy, *el aguante* (the ability to hold up well even in the face of abuse), and *la concha* (a thick hard shell that will not budge, no matter how much effort is made to get through it to the person) are either Mexican sociocultural virtues, or realistic ways of coping, or else, and at least, approved ways of defending oneself from the stresses of life.

Further, the prevalent religion in Mexico and the pre-Cortesian view agree that "this is a valley of tears," and there is a prevalent easy adjustment of the Mexican to tragedy, even to death. The same can be said about a chronic illness or deformity. There is also a widespread use of the expression *ni modo* (said with a gigantic shrug of the shoulders), which means: "what can anyone do, there is no way." Further, the widespread use of proverbs, stories, and jokes of a quasi-stoic philosophy, as well as strong fatalistic attitudes, is an example of a well-integrated and well-learned philosophy that the very best and the fairest way, to others and to oneself—the righteous and the virtuous way to deal with stress—is passivity. Here we may tell the often-repeated story of a man found by another at the bottom of a well, crying out and complaining. He was asked about his suffering. The answer was a long and sad story of how bandits had come to his farm, had killed his wife, children, mother, and grandmother, had taken away all of his possessions, had burned his house, and had left him for dead after stabbing him forty times. To which the rescuer said: "How terrible! But don't you hurt horribly from your wounds?" The Mexican replied, "No, they don't hurt; they only hurt when I laugh." I hope this joke is self-explanatory.

The prevalent American philosophy, on the other hand, is to deal with stress actively. Americans make a virtue of this and consider it the best possible way to face reality. For the American, life is lived best in constant activity. Here is a culture where self-esteem decays if one is idle, as demonstrated by the studies of Paul Lazarsfeld and P. Eisenberg.[3] But, since the best way, the virtuous way, the righteous way, even the fair way in dealing with others is to face stress actively, Americans have a hard time with death, chronic illness, deformity, poverty, and beggars. In a cross-cultural research project that we are in the process of carrying out under a grant from the Foundations' Fund for Research in Psychiatry (FFRP) in collaboration with Dr. Wayne H. Holtzman of the University of Texas, the plan has been to include a series of T.A.T. pictures showing some of the situations we feel can demonstrate the existence of the cross-cultural dichotomy.

In the paper cited,[4] it was further hypothesized that there would be a large number of differences between cultures that held opposing views about the proper way of dealing with stress. The following was pointed out: "Psychologically, the AES [active subjects] should value conflict, competition, action, aggressiveness, equality, individual freedom, opportunity, independence, informality, content rather than form, and pragmatism. . . . PES [passive subjects] should value harmony, protection, dependence, cooperation, idleness, prescribed

---

[3] Paul Lazarsfeld, "An Unemployed Village," *Character and Personality* 1 (1932): 147–151; P. Eisenberg and Paul Lazarsfeld, "The Psychological Effects of Unemployment," *Psychological Bulletin* 35 (1938): 358–390.

[4] Essay 7.

roles, formality, form rather than content, and platonic philosophy. Psychodynamically, for the same amount of frustration, the PES will produce less aggression." Psychosomatically, we hypothesize hypertension, stomach ulcers, and coronaries for active endurers, and, psychiatrically, more hypochondriasis and hysteria for passive endurers. Socially, more racial intolerance and discrimination are to be expected in active endurers, more intolerance also for social deviants, more mental illness, physical illness, and alcoholism.

In passive endurers there will be more economic exploitation, greater economic distance between the rich and the poor, and greater personal emotional and economic exploitation of one individual by another (the *aguante*). Criminologically, it was felt that more crime for economic gain would be found in AES; and, in PES, more crime after reaching the limits of passive endurance and in emotional problems. In religion, Catholicism, it was said, is mainly a PES philosophy and Protestantism an AES philosophy. In economic philosophies, capitalism and Marxism-Leninism both would be considered AES philosophies. "The second is, however, a far more extreme reaction to PES, more often leading to violence (the struggle of the classes), and, in practice, ending in a greater imposition of stress on individuals, who still, characteristically, endure it passively." A series of other sociocultural and international differences were enumerated to point out the usefulness of the passive-active transcultural dichotomy.

Application to Mental Health

But one of the most important consequences of this active-passive dichotomy is the application of the concept to mental health.

In the FFRP project referred to above, it was proposed—as one of the objects of the research—to find the differences in the style of coping with stress of Mexican and American school children. Later, after a highly stimulating conversation with Dr. Robert F. Peck, it was decided that this passive-active cross-cultural dichotomy would be of greater interest to mental health if combined with the concepts of coping (as used by Lois B. Murphy)[5] and of defense (as understood

[5] Lois B. Murphy, *The Widening World of Childhood.*

in psychoanalytic psychodynamics). As a result of this conversation, we have come to visualize the problem of mental health in what appears to us to be a more comprehensive and understanding approach. That is, we feel that mental health may sometimes be gained in other ways than by actively "facing reality," as has so often been implied on the American scene. It is possible to deal with *either reality*, the environmental or the inner reality, with at least two general patterns of behavior, which, depending upon the problems and sometimes for the same problem, may both be healthy. That is, mental health may come about by actively doing something about it or by passively accepting what comes. This has led to the realization that defense may also be dichotomous and that the same person may use both passive and active defenses.

Within the American culture, there seems to be a defined trend to make activity synonymous with efficiency, health, and even fairness and righteousness. This appears to be so prevalent that passive coping will often be considered at least as wishy-washy and more often as dishonest or as unhealthy. Thus it is no wonder that, in Mexico, the active extravaganzas of American tourists may often be considered inadequate, unfair, somewhat crazy (*esos gringos locos*, "those crazy Americans"), and, therefore, even unhealthy and psychopathic. It is very difficult to forget the reactions of a delightful, friendly, and efficient American secretary, who was typing for me the items of a test in which children were portrayed as coping with stress either actively or passively. I cannot forget her quite consistent reactions as she typed. To the active coping with stress she would exclaim, "That is Johnny, that is my boy!" and to the passive coping she would exclaim just as enthusiastically, "Oh! He is cheating, that Gaspar is cheating!"

At any rate, it is felt that research in these areas will discover that many healthy mechanisms of coping and defense in one culture are considered inadequate in the other. By this token, and by the restriction imposed by these all-inclusive and—it can be seen—powerful sociocultural premises of activity and passivity, humans appear to be restricted in their spontaneity from using more and better ways of coping with stress. We may conclude, therefore, that active cultures would gain a great deal if they were able to accept as valid and good, in certain problems, the ways of passive copers. On the other hand, passive cultures would increase their ability to deal with stress —and therefore their mental health—by accepting ways of dealing with stress actively, above and beyond the powerful sociocultural restrictions, allowing themselves to increase their armamentarium for dealing with the multiple and ever-present stresses of life.

9. Problems and Preliminary Results of Sociopsychological Research in Mexico

Introduction

From the little work, published and unpublished, that is being done in Mexico of a social-psychological nature, I am going to select for this paper the work that I and a group of students and colleagues have been doing. The selection is made not necessarily on the basis of its value but on the basis of its relevance to the goals and to the means enumerated and summarized in a clear and, in my opinion, perceptive and pertinent fashion in the general report by Henri Tajfel and in the proposal by Herbert C. Kelman.[1]

Our very first studies belong to a descriptive level. They were

NOTE. This paper was presented at the Seventy-third Annual Meeting of the American Psychological Association, September, 1965.

[1] Henri Tajfel, "Problems of International Cooperation in Social Psychological Research Concerned with New and Developing Countries" (mimeographed, 1964); Herbert C. Kelman, "Social-Psychological Research in Developing Countries" (mimeographed, 1965). Dr. Tajfel, of Oxford University, wrote to 256 scientists in fifty countries, in 1964, asking about the potential value of sociopsychological research with respect to the problems of developing countries. His paper gives the results of this inquiry. Dr. Kelman, a former president of the Society for the Psychological Study of Social Issues, undertook the gigantic task

directed toward determining the attitudes of the Mexicans of Mexico City, and they probed into such generalized topics of social psychology as the roles of the different members of the family, the roles of the sexes in the family and in the society, etc. Underlying these studies was a thinking that appeared bent on integrating anthropological, sociological, and psychodynamic concepts, implemented, however, by some of the sociopsychological technology of sampling and attitude testing. The research teams at this stage were integrated by this investigator and some enterprising students, with no budget for salaries or even for the paper and the printing of questionnaires, etc.

One highlight of these studies was that the statements in the questionnaires were designed to confirm or reject hypotheses that I could state probably only because I grew up in what may be considered a typical Mexican family, and because at twenty-four I had the chance to live, for four years, in a strikingly different socioculture. At any rate, I was quite certain of the way the answers would turn out to the first few questions that we asked. First hesitatingly, and later self-assuredly, we called the statements in the questionnaires "Mexican sociocultural premises." In one of the better studies, we obtained the results that may be seen in Tables 9-1 to 9-3. Several good things came out of these studies:

1. What we and others found in Mexico City residents in several samples[2] has been found recently by Dr. Luis Lara Tapia in Spanish-speaking Otomies and in non-Spanish-speaking Otomies in the state of Tlaxcala in Mexico.[3]

---

of organizing an international conference of about sixty social scientists, predominantly from developing countries, to encourage the development of the social sciences with respect to the study of the psychosocial problems of development. Results of this conference are reported in *Social Psychological Research in Developing Countries*, edited by John Delamater et al., *Journal of Social Issues* 24, no. 2 (1968).

[2] Essay 4; R. Díaz-Guerrero, "Una escala factorial de premisas histórico-socioculturales de la familia mexicana," *Interamerican Journal of Psychology* 6, nos. 3–4 (1972): 235–244; Carmen Rojo I., "El cambio de actitudes: Algunas consideraciones teóricas y un experimento psicosocial" (unpublished).

[3] Luis Lara Tapia and María Luisa Morales, "Premisas socioculturales en tres comunidades indígenas de Tlaxcala" (mimeographed).

Table 9-1
Sociocultural Premises about the Mother and
the Feminine Role

	All-Male Schools	Males in Mixed Schools	Females in Mixed Schools	All-Female Schools
Number of Subjects	172	110	88	102
	(%)	(%)	(%)	(%)
1. It is not right for a married woman to work outside of her home.	61.1	54.5	36.3	48.0
2. The place for women is in the home.	84.3	87.1	89.8	73.5
3. You should never question the word of your mother.	83.0	75.5	87.5	82.4
4. A woman should be a virgin until she marries.	83.1	69.0	75.0	82.6
5. Young women should not go out alone at night with men.	60.4	62.7	60.4	72.6
6. The majority of men like submissive women.	75.3	62.0	71.2	66.8
7. All men desire to marry a virgin.	81.4	63.6	65.9	75.5
8. Little girls should be seen but not heard.	67.4	62.7	70.2	76.4
9. For me the mother is the dearest person in the world.	89.6	90.0	95.4	88.3
10. The majority of girls would like to be like their mothers.	61.0	47.2	64.9	72.0
11. A good wife never questions the behavior of her husband.	79.6	77.1	74.0	83.2
12. The majority of Mexican women make many sacrifices.	55.2	61.0	70.4	50.0
13. Women need to be protected.	90.6	80.0	86.3	81.4
14. A good wife is always loyal to her husband.	92.4	80.0	84.0	94.0

2. Departing from our work, Drs. E. D. Maldonado Sierra, R. Fernández Marina, and Richard D. Trent of the Puerto Rican Institute of Psychiatry have found, in several studies, a very similar pattern of sociocultural premises.[4]

[4] E. D. Maldonado Sierra, Richard D. Trent, and R. Fernández Marina, "Three Basic Themes in Mexican and Puerto Rican Family Values," *Journal of Social*

Table 9-2
Sociocultural Premises about the Father and
the Masculine Role

	All-Male Schools	Males in Mixed Schools	Females in Mixed Schools	All-Female Schools
Number of Subjects	172	110	88	102
	(%)	(%)	(%)	(%)
1. You should never question the word of your father.	84.2	72.0	75.0	74.2
2. It is more important to respect your father than to love him.	65.2	64.5	69.3	42.2
3. The majority of Mexican men feel superior to women.	66.2	56.4	60.2	63.8
4. All men should be *complete* men ("real" men).	75.0	77.3	62.5	60.8
5. All boys should have self-confidence.	69.7	62.7	73.8	76.4
6. A man should wear the pants in the family.	84.3	69.0	62.5	72.0
7. The majority of boys would like to be like their fathers.	74.4	—	58.0	80.4

Table 9-3
Sociocultural Premises about Both Parents and the Family

	All-Male Schools	Males in Mixed Schools	Females in Mixed Schools	All-Female Schools
Number of Subjects	172	110	88	102
	(%)	(%)	(%)	(%)
1. It is not right for a married woman to work outside of her home.	61.1	54.5	36.3	48.0
2. A man who is not a "real" man dishonors his family.	92.4	80.0	84.0	94.0
3. You should always be loyal to your family.	90.1	86.4	90.9	90.2
4. A girl should always obey her parents.	87.2	87.2	94.3	93.1
5. A son should always obey his parents.	87.8	89.0	87.4	83.4
6. A person should always respect his parents.	96.5	94.6	95.5	96.0
7. A woman who commits adultery dishonors her family.	74.9	60.9	55.7	70.6
8. Small children should be seen but not heard.	78.0	72.7	79.5	79.4

3. More recently, the consistency of these sociocultural premises (SCPs) is being used by some students as a starting point for studies of attitude change.[5]

4. These studies have helped our students to develop awareness of their specific socioculture and of some of the contradictions that they as adolescents sometimes live in.

This kind of approach is also being used at the present time to study regional differences or similarities, and it may be useful in the process of producing national awareness.

Beginnings of Transcultural Research

In spite of the extraordinary similarity of Mexican and Puerto Rican sociocultural beliefs, there were quantitative differences. Somehow, as a result of this, the idea of trying to establish differences between Mexicans and Americans became more and more attractive. Here we had splendid—and totally different—sociocultures that were kissing each other along a very long border. Dr. Robert F. Peck and this writer became codirectors of these studies. The Hogg Foundation for Mental Health paid for work by research assistants, secretaries, and tabulators, and for material expenses. Strict codirection produced questionnaires mindful of differences across the border. Studies of the meaning of certain words, such as *respect* and *love*,[6] of the relationship between the assignation of respect and social status,[7] and of the reciprocal attitudes and expectations of males and females in both countries revealed a large number of differences between Mexicans and Americans. The highlight here is that the strict collaboration between researchers in the two cultures—which produced a number of reciprocal cultural shocks—led to the finding of differences meaningful within each society and understandable across cultures.

Psychology 48 (1958): 167–181; idem, "Neurosis and Traditional Family Beliefs in Puerto Rico," *International Journal of Social Psychiatry* 6 (1960): 237–246.

[5] Rojo I., "El cambio de actitudes."

[6] Essay 5; Robert F. Peck and R. Díaz-Guerrero, "The Meaning of Love in Mexico and the United States," *American Psychologist* 17 (1962): 329.

[7] Essay 6.

Cross-cultural Research Takes Root in Mexico

Beyond determining somewhat quantitatively the main beliefs about the family roles and the sex roles in family and society, the sociocultural-premise studies and the cross-cultural studies did not appear—at least at the beginning—to give us any idea about what we should do next. We were haunted by the need of establishing a more systematic theoretical approach to understand what we had already found and to lead the way for future studies. At the same time, many problems of a practical nature, such as those that Henri Tajfel insists lead to—and, I feel, sometimes force—theoretical insights,[8] kept knocking at our doors. Such problems included the standardization of mental tests for Mexico, the determination of obvious needs for the education of the population, the development of personality characteristics, capacities, abilities, and cognitive patterns in school children, etc. The chance to study this all properly came when Dr. Wayne H. Holtzman started a large study of personality and cognitive development in school children in Austin, Texas, and enticed us to write a project along similar lines. The project, entitled "Personality Development of Mexican School Children," received a grant from the Foundations' Fund for Research in Psychiatry.

Highlights of this study, begun in January, 1964, are as follows:

1. It was the first time that the principal investigator was paid to do research.[9]

2. It provided an opportunity to give advanced research training and experience to a small core of graduate students and psychologists, thereby increasing future resources available for research.

3. There was an opportunity to literally "worry systematically" about the relevant socioeconomic variables of the population of Mexico City by carrying on preliminary demographic surveys about the population to be studied, that is, public school children, children in school housing projects, children in private schools, etc.

[8] Tajfel, "Problems of International Cooperation."

[9] Independent professional incomes of the writer and his wife had permitted all previous research to be done without pay. This is not possible for the majority of psychologists and social psychologists in the developing countries. In most cases, even the very first trials at research will have to be remunerated in some way.

4. It was possible to utilize this demographic evidence in the selection of samples of children for intensive psychological study.

5. There was an opportunity to investigate the developmental aspects of perception and related cognitive functioning and other personality characteristics and abilities in children and adolescents, with specific concern for intracultural variation in the urban sample.

6. There was an opportunity to systematically evaluate cross-cultural differences in psychological development between comparable school children of urban centers of Mexico and the United States.

7. There was an opportunity to standardize approximately ten selected psychological tests for normal, socially stable urban school children in Mexico City.

8. It was possible to pay research assistants, graduate students in training, and bilingual secretaries and to obtain computer services, materials, etc.

9. The study provided an incentive to develop further our theoretical ideas regarding cross-cultural differences and to test them by observing the results obtained in each one of the measurements applied cross-culturally.

10. There was an opportunity to develop new tests in the way that will be explained in the next section.

11. This was the first splendid opportunity for a phase that is indispensable wherever cross-cultural research is contemplated: the development of tooling, that is, instruments of measurement that will be usable for cross-cultural comparisons in the different countries.

It is precisely in regard to the last highlight that we should refer to the opportunity that was offered to us by Dr. Charles E. Osgood to develop for Mexico the native version of the Semantic Differential. This was another of those cases where only the research assistant and the materials and secretarial work were paid for. But the importance of the tool, already in development autochthonously in sixteen different countries, made it an attractive operation. We are happy to report that the Mexican Semantic Differential is now in existence and ready to be used for cross-cultural studies.

Also relevant to tooling and training is the more recent contact that we were able to establish with the Western Behavioral Sciences Institute. About fourteen members of the institute's research team came to Mexico and trained a team of Mexican social psychologists and social scientists in the carrying out of internation simulations.

In both the last cases, the Mexican groups that have participated in the activity looked forward to this type of training partially because they already had a number of hypotheses they wanted to see tested in the sort of social-psychological "action research" that simulation represents. This was particularly true for those who had previously used only questionnaires and other testing materials.

Theory and Practice in Social Psychology

It appears to me that the more specific practical applications there are, the better the theory has to be. Thinking as a physician, as a psychiatrist, and as a social psychologist, through experiences and contradictions related elsewhere,[10] we arrived at a sociocultural premise that we felt might be in command of the ways in which people of different countries deal with the omnipresent problem of stress.[11] People in some cultures do something about the stresses that they face; they modify the environment in an attempt to handle the stress. We called these the active endurers of stress. People in other cultures do not do anything about the stress; instead, they accept it, modifying not the environment but themselves. We called these the passive endurers of stress. Influenced by Lois Murphy's concept of coping,[12] we decided that among the goals of the research to be done in collaboration with Dr. Wayne H. Holtzman it would be useful to include the possibility of developing tests intended to measure the style of coping with stress in the two cultures.[13]

[10] R. Díaz-Guerrero, "Socio-Cultural and Psychodynamic Processes in Adolescent Transition and Mental Health," in Problems of Youth: Transition to Adulthood in a Changing World, ed. Muzafer Sherif and Carolyn W. Sherif.

[11] For a definition of the term stress, see "México en la cultura," Novedades, 3d ser., no. 837 (April 4, 1965).

[12] Lois B. Murphy, The Widening World of Childhood.

[13] R. Díaz-Guerrero, "Personality Development of Mexican School Children: A Research Proposal Submitted to the Foundations' Fund for Research in Psychiatry," Anuario de Psicología 3 (1964): 99–109.

Later, for a conference in Chicago,[14] Dr. Robert F. Peck and the writer developed a research design in which the active and passive styles of dealing with stress were combined with the concept of coping and with the concept of defense as understood in psychoanalytic psychodynamics. As a result, we had a two-by-two design for the study of patterns of coping and defense cross-culturally. Further, as layers of the cake there were constructs of possibly stressing experiences like authority, task accomplishment, anxiety, anger, interpersonal relations. The design was, therefore, to confront the problem of the cross-cultural difference of coping and defense in connection with the above-enumerated series of stressors. This rather simple design was discussed and, after broadening and modification, became a seven-nation project that has recently been given a grant by the United States Department of Education. The project, entitled "Coping Style and Achievement: A Cross-National Study of School Children," will try to determine relationships between style of coping and defense, measures of achievement, sociometry, intelligence, and many other variables.[15]

Highlights of this research are as follows:

1. The team of students that I have had in training from the inception of the Holtzman–Díaz-Guerrero program of research have become fairly convinced that it is possible to have a local Mexican psychology that will study the problems of the Mexican and that will find its own solutions for the problems of its people.

2. A crusader spirit has spread among other students of psychology, and a large amount of interest in more rigorous methodologies has spread like a flame. People at the Electronic Computer Center and at other schools of the National University of Mexico, as well as individuals in other universities, have started to show an interest in the scientific methodologies of social psychology.

3. We ourselves have been modified, together with some of the

14 The Cross-National Conference on Childhood and Adolescence, organized by Dr. Robert D. Hess of the Committee on Human Development of the University of Chicago, held February 21–28, 1964.

15 Robert F. Peck et al., "Coping Style and Achievement: A Cross-National Study of School Children" (mimeographed, 1965).

Table 9-4

Motivations for Working: Paired Comparison Study

Items	Frequency of Preference of Each Stimulus over All the Rest				
	Social Classes			Total	Sum of Upper and Middle
	Upper	Middle	Lower		
1. I work because there is no other alternative.	111	131	184	426	242
2. I work to demonstrate my personal ability.	165	178	165	508	343
3. I work for the satisfaction of using my skills.	226	199	170	595	425
4. I work for the money I am paid.	205	205	194	604	410
5. I work so thatt Mexico will progress.	209	220	214	643	429
6. I work because I like to work.	226	227	198	651	453
7. I work because it is my duty.	241	271	245	757	512
8. I work to make my way in life.	269	252	271	792	521
9. I work to give my children an education.	306	300	300	906	606
10. I work to support my family.	316	309	297	922	625

Number of subjects: 153 (51 per social class)

first rigorously trained psychologists of Mexico, to the extent that several of our laboratory demonstrations in experimental psychology and other subjects are now taking on the flavor of the paired comparison study, the preliminary results of which I am presenting to you in Table 9-4.[16]

Would anyone in the United States anticipate such attitudinal motivations for work to prevail in a similar sample of fathers? The results shown in this table should be taken into account by those who are eagerly attempting to motivate and stimulate the Mexican worker by means of approaches developed for other cultures.[17]

[16] This study, in all its stages, was carried out with the enthusiastic cooperation of a hundred students in the experimental-psychology course of the evening school of the College of Psychology of the National University of Mexico in 1965.

[17] Comparison of the results shown in Tables 9-1–9-3, obtained from adolescents, with those in Table 9-4, obtained from Mexican fathers, reveals that the adolescents predominantly want to obey and respect their fathers and that the fathers predominantly want to work in order to provide for the education of their

Looking toward the Future

The final highlight is, therefore, the confidence of the social psychologists that the people in a developing country may be led to a higher productivity, etc., by utilizing motivations, incentives, understandings, and standardizations that may be very different from those that are used in the developed countries. The further realization has been reached that perhaps it is possible to become industrialized and economically productive without necessarily falling prey to some of the abnormal deviations of those developed countries where the sociocultural premises have, perhaps accidentally, followed the economic development. The social psychologist of the developing country may perhaps think that his society may avoid such terrible problems as juvenile delinquency, increased suicides, suicide in children, high divorce rates, discrimination against minorities, etc. All of these are such glowing and fantastic possibilities that the psychologist of the developing country might find himself highly motivated in his research. Not absent from his motivation may be the idea that perhaps he can teach the psychologists and the people of the developed countries a trick or two in the game of dealing with the stresses of life.

After all, he may have suddenly come to realize that people in his country do not need perhaps to *change* so much—this may be a wrong perception originating from the developed countries—it may merely be necessary to encourage their growth.

Let us then finish with a question. What are the advantages for social-psychological research in the developing countries if it addresses itself to the problem of the growth of a group or a nation rather than the problem of how to change a group or how to change a nation?

---

children. These and other results (see Essay 7; R. Díaz-Guerrero, "Socio-Cultural and Psychodynamic Processes") have led us to perceive the Mexican socioculture as one whose philosophy of life is dominated by a passive-affiliative-interdependent orientation and in which success and profit and productivity are often sought, not for themselves or for individualistic enjoyment, but for what they mean in terms of others (the family, etc.) or in terms of a symbol (Mexico). This is in extreme contrast with the active-autonomous philosophy of life and individualistically oriented concept of profit and success that we believe to be the dominant philosophy of the American.

10. Exploring Dimensions in Socioeconomic Development

Let us start with an incredible series of statements about what work is and what to do about it. They are all Mexican sayings. "Honest work will ruin your back." "Idleness is the mother of a most wonderful life." "If drinking interferes with your work, stop working." "Work is sacred; don't touch it." These and similar expressions of the folkloric wisdom of the Mexican people have become widespread all over Mexico, and I am willing to bet that every Mexican sounds or resounds to these expressions at an average of once a month. What does this mean? Is it that Mexicans are "lazy, no-good people"? Is it that work for them is such a dismal experience that they must forever defend themselves from it? Is it that the idea of work in the abstract is something that carries extremely negative connotations? Do these expressions mean that there is no way to make Mexicans work? Does it simply attest to an excellent sense of humor? Since I am raising the questions, I suppose that you are somewhat anticipat-

NOTE. This was an invited paper at the Ninety-fourth Annual Forum of the National Conference on Social Welfare, May, 1967.

ing that I may have some of the answers. But we should, in the very first place, indicate that, in spite of the intense efforts of "modernization" that have taken place in Mexico and in Latin America, as in many other developing areas of the world, there is very little fact and even very little capable opinion that can bear upon these questions.

Let me tell you now that from this moment on I will be speaking about Mexicans instead of Latin Americans at large, because we have a little more information about them in regard to the problems that we are going to be discussing and also because we have a greater amount of comparative information concerning Mexicans and Americans. I would like you to remember, however, that often the things I ascribe to Mexicans may be extended to other Latin Americans, even if this is not always the case.

Now let us return to the interesting Mexican sayings and to the questions that they raise, and let us assume that we should answer affirmatively to all of the negative implications, that is to say, Mexicans are lazy, Mexicans cannot be made to work, Mexicans are interested in the siesta and in the fiesta and nothing else, etc.

If we did this, we would have to immediately face the reality that Mexico has been increasing its national product at a rate two to three times above what was hoped for, by most programs of economic development for Latin America.

Now, confronted with this fact, what do we do, what do we say? Is it possible that these Mexicans who are increasing their national product at this incredible rate are the same Mexicans who have produced and are still creating new sayings as derogatory as those above about work?

The fact is that these rebellious Mexicans are working extremely hard. Now, why are they working? This is our second set of questions. Do they want to become individual successes? Do they want to show everyone else that they are better than the others? Are they competing among themselves to the point of "dog eats dog"? Are they interested somewhat egotistically and specifically in the development of their own individual capacities and potentialities? Do they want to live up to the González? Are there any other dimensions that might explain their high productivity and motivation to work?

Let us say that, in regard to this overwhelming number of un-answered questions, we have been able, at least, to develop a certain pattern of thinking, and we are at the present time busily exploring some of the potentially meaningful angles of the total problem in the hope that the larger puzzle may come to be easier to put together.

But now let us put to one side what we have been talking about, not because we are going to leave it to one side for the rest of this talk, but because we are going to be talking about something different that we hope to tie in with the previous discussion later.

Let me state first that I do not consider, nor do I want to consider, the problem of socioeconomic development as an isolated feature or as something that can be handled independently and apart from such considerations as those embodied in the approaches of social welfare or even, if you press the point, in the philosophy of humanitarianism. I am convinced that—perhaps not in the short, perhaps not even in the long, but certainly in the longer run—greater efficiency, produc-tivity, and creativity will come from a fairly well-adjusted society— and I mean an emotionally adjusted society, rather than one that is economically adjusted to the point of accumulation of so much money that it cannot use it.

Let me say it in fewer words: I believe that "economic theory and practice" with regard to development should very much go hand in hand with studies, just as intensive, of the modifications that such theory and practice produce in the "theory and practice of living," and vice versa; that is to say, we should be very aware that the theory and practice of living may have a tremendous impact on economic development, and particularly so in developing nations.

And now, as an introduction to the effects that in Mexico the theory and practice of living may have upon the theory and practice of economic development, let me make a very shocking statement: I believe that Mexicans, and in this case I want to include specifically all Latin Americans, may have always worked more, and are, par-ticularly at the present, working more per working person than Americans. Let me give you a concrete example of what I am trying to say. Let us assume that we could develop an index of the teaching efficiency of teachers. Let us call it for the sake of big beautiful words a "national annual index of efficiency per teacher." Let us say that we figured it out in this way. We take the number of children taught per teacher, we take the amount of knowledge gained by those children, we take into account the amount of money in its relative value that the teacher receives, and then we determine the yearly amount of knowledge imparted by each teacher over the amount of money earned. I am thoroughly convinced that Mexican teachers would come far ahead of American teachers in this type of index. In other words, they would work more; they would impart far more knowledge for less money, and under more difficult conditions. This is not, believe me, an atypical example. Now let us assume that you grant me that what I am saying is true. What is far more interesting than this is the series of questions that will be immediately forthcoming. If it is true that Mexicans and Latin Americans are working more for less pay and under worse conditions than Americans, what on earth, what possible reason can possibly lead them into this impossible activity?

Let me stop here once more and warn you that I am now using "American logic." Americans would certainly find it almost impossible—in general, of course—to work a great deal for little money and under harsh working conditions. It is, therefore, even more urgent to try and find an answer for these questions. What possible mystique, what possible motives are leading Mexicans and Latin Americans to work this hard and under those conditions? And now, to show the relevance and the importance that these questions may have even for Americans, let us ask a question: What would make Americans work very hard for little money and under harsh conditions? There is a body of young people of which Americans may be very proud, the Peace Corps. What are their motives? Let me tell you that most of the citizens of Mexico are, in that sense, Peace Corps workers.

Perhaps I am beginning to succeed in providing an adequate frame or reference to my statements, and maybe I have helped the audience into an adequate frame of mind for what I will say next. Socioeconomic development is deeply intertwined in Mexico—and, I believe, in most developing countries—with what we may call sociocultural values. To these sociocultural values I have given a less controversial name and provided an operational definition; I call them *sociocultural premises*. I have the feeling that an understanding of the sociocultural premises for each country, and perhaps for each group, will help tremendously in making the decisions that are needed for increased organization and efficiency of what is already a very hard-working and large group of human beings in action in Mexico and in Latin America. I cannot—within the limits of this paper—tell you what the sociocultural premises are or in what ways I and others have already been able to find some interesting differences between Mexicans and Americans in regard to them.[1] I am going to pass right away to some data that may serve as illustrations for some of the problems that we have been dealing with here today, and then we can make some relevant closing remarks and conclusions.

Let us look at Table 10-1, which portrays the "affective meaning" of the concept *work* in four different countries. Work for the U.S.

[1] G. V. Coelho et al., "A Cross-Cultural Assessment of Coping Behavior: Student TAT Responses of Competent Adolescents in Maryland and Puerto Rico" (mimeographed, 1964); Essay 7; R. Díaz-Guerrero, "Socio-Cultural and Psychodynamic Processes in Adolescent Transition and Mental Health," in *Problems of Youth: Transition to Adulthood in a Changing World*, ed. Muzafer Sherif and Carolyn W. Sherif; R. Díaz-Guerrero et al., "Simposio de estudios transculturales del desarrollo infantil en México y en los Estados Unidos en relación a factores de personalidad, cognición y clase social," in *Memorias del X Congreso Interamericano de Psicología*, ed. C. F. Hereford and L. Natalicio, pp. 121–164; C. F. Hereford et al., "A Cross-Cultural Comparison of the Active-Passive Dimension of Social Attitudes," *Interamerican Journal of Psychology* 1, no. 1 (March 1967): 33–39; C. F. Hereford, "La dimensión actividad-pasividad en México y los Estados Unidos" (paper presented at the Primer Congreso Nacional de Psicología, Jalapa, Ver., Mexico, 1967; to be published by Imprenta Universitaria, UNAM); Robert F. Peck et al., "Symposium on Problem-Solving Styles in Children: A Cross-National Study," in *Memorias del X Congreso Interamericano de Psicología*, ed. C. F. Hereford and L. Natalicio, pp. 223–268; Robert F. Peck et al., "Coping Style and Achievement: A Cross-National Study of School Children" (mimeographed, 1965); R. Díaz-Guerrero and Robert F. Peck, "Estilo de confrontación y aprovechamiento: Un programa de investigación," *Revista Interamericana de Psicología* 1967, no. 1: 127–136.

Table 10-1
Affective Meaning of Work

Industrialized Countries			
	Evaluation	Potency	Activity
United States	.822	1.441	.171
Sweden	.881	.694	.706
Developing Countries			
	Evaluation	Potency	Activity
Mexico (Yucatán)[a]	1.147	.977	1.264
Mexico (Mexico City)	1.469	1.025	.631
India	.950	.800	−.569

NOTE. The numbers represent the mean affective connotation in a scale from +3 to −3, with 0 being the neutral point. Data were obtained from a current study by Charles E. Osgood et al., "An Atlas of Meanings," in which Mexico participates with sixteen other nations. The study is done with support from the Human Ecology Fund and the National Institute of Mental Health. *Standardized composite scores* derived from the mean and the standard deviation for each dimension (Evaluation, Potency, Activity) change the relations as used in our discussion but maintain and often dramatize the cross-cultural difference.

[a] These data are from a study by William May.

sample means something that is "O.K."—no great enthusiasm here—quite powerful, but almost neutral in regard to the perceived activity that seems to be required. For Mexicans it is a little more O.K. than for Americans, but certainly less powerful, although it does require a good deal of activity. In India it is O.K., less powerful than in the United States, and perceived as requiring a certain degree of passivity; and in Sweden it is as O.K. as in the United States, is perceived as least powerful, and requires an amount of activity halfway between the small amount perceived by the American sample and the high activity perceived by the Mexicans.

Let us, for the sake of argument, interpret the results for Mexico and the United States as substantiating my previous statement that Mexicans work more (more activity) for less money (less power in work) and still see work just as kindly as Americans.

But what is inescapable from this table is that *work* has a different meaning for each of the four samples.

Table 10-2
Motivations for Working: Paired Comparison Study

	Frequency of Preference of Each Stimulus over All the Rest				
	Social Classes				Sum of Upper and
Items	Upper	Middle	Lower	Total	Middle
1. I work because there is no other alternative.	111	131	184	426	242
2. I work to demonstrate my personal ability.	165	178	165	508	343
3. I work for the satisfaction of using my skills.	226	199	170	595	425
4. I work for the money I am paid.	205	205	194	604	410
5. I work so that Mexico will progress.	209	220	214	643	429
6. I work because I like to work.	226	227	198	651	453
7. I work because it is my duty.	241	271	245	757	512
8. I work to make my way in life.	269	252	271	792	521
9. I work to give my children an education.	306	300	300	906	606
10. I work to support my family.	316	309	297	922	625

Number of subjects: 153 (51 per social class)

Let us move on to Table 10-2. With the help of our students, we carried out a very simple research to try to find out—in this case only for Mexicans—some of the reasons why they work. In Table 10-2 you will see the results. As you can see from a perusal of this table, the kinds of motivations that appear to be most important for Mexican working people from all socioeconomic classes, the main reasons they give us for working are not the work itself, not their own individualized getting ahead, not the use of their own potentialities, but are often reasons of affiliative connotation. They are working for someone else, they are working for the family, they are working for the children, and they are often working because they consider that to work is a duty that must be fulfilled. This goes well with their generalized philosophy of enduring and adapting themselves to the demands of their environment. Although we don't have similar results for American parents, what we know from previous studies in America indicates that some of the most highly motivating factors for Americans to work are, of course, to "get somewhere in life," to succeed, to put to work their own potentialities, to do the work because work is its own reward, etc. More studies should be carried out, but these results suggest that, beyond the fact that work is perceived differently by different groups, motivation for work may vary too.

And now we have Table 10-3. The curious results reported for American and Mexican students indicate a very different set of sociocultural premises regarding work, the speed with which work should be carried out, the better way to carry on with fellow workers, etc. These and other results, some published, some in the process of being published, have led us to feel that Americans in their everyday life could be best described as active, optimistic, autonomous, efficiency-conscious, competitive, self-sufficient, aggressive, and tense; and Mexicans as passive, fatalistic, affiliative, interdependent, cooperative, humble, obedient, and relaxed.

The simple illustrations in Tables 10-1 to 10-3 suggest that work is perceived differently by different groups, that the motivation to work may be quite different, and that the means to get the things done, through cooperation or competition, may be also quite different. Further, different approaches to the whole problem may be just as productive as or more productive than the American way. Fundamentally, it is not necessarily true that "business is business"; very humane motivations may enter, and some of these foreign schemes on how to do work may be healthier than the American scheme from the humanistic point of view. There is much to be learned about mental health and work from other societies outside the United States. Thus, the great fun that Mexicans appear to have berating work does not reduce their evaluation of work, certainly does not interfere with their ability to work, and may help them to endure work better. Further, their philosophy that life is to be endured rather than enjoyed may pay good dividends, not only in respect to the ability to work longer without interruption, but also in respect to life in general. If we had a representative sample of Americans and of Mexicans and judges rated their obvious degree of happiness and enjoyment of life, I would bet that the Mexicans would come out ahead of the Ameri-

Table 10-3
Sociocultural Premises

	United States				Mexico			
	Male		Female		Male		Female	
	O	R	O	R	O	R	O	R
1. a. Cooperation is better than competition to achieve results.	10	71	18	52	42	97	32	64
b. Competition is better than cooperation to achieve results.	11	42	9	37	5	28	16	23
2. a. One must fight when the rights of the family are threatened.	6	28	4	18	22	89	31	59
b. One must fight when the rights of the individual are threatened.	15	84	24	70	22	38	15	32
3. a. I prefer a work partner who is friendly.	10	58	8	47	26	73	35	60
b. I prefer a work partner who is hard working.	10	52	20	42	18	53	15	24
4. a. Competition stimulates achievement.	13	49	16	43	15	22	6	23
b. The best results are achieved by exchanging ideas and working cooperatively with your coworkers.	8	62	12	47	32	103	42	62
5. a. It is better to be slow rather than fast.	6	27	8	26	28	82	35	50
b. It is better to be fast rather than slow.	15	82	18	63	19	45	13	36
6. a. Strike while the iron is hot.	17	83	24	63	27	70	20	30
b. Everything comes to him who waits.	4	22	3	25	18	56	28	58
7. a. Everything at its own time.	9	51	15	47	31	82	35	65
b. The sooner you get the things the better.	12	63	13	43	13	44	12	33
8. a. Never think of the future—it comes soon enough.	1	24	6	27	21	32	21	34
b. The future holds all our rewards.	20	86	20	59	25	93	29	53

| | United States | | | | Mexico | | | |
| | Male | | Female | | Male | | Female | |
	O	R	O	R	O	R	O	R
9. *a.* If you are in an earthquake it will feel better to run.	14	51	16	34	9	11	9	10
b. If you are in an earthquake it will feel better to stay put.	7	59	12	54	35	115	40	77
10. *a.* Life is to be enjoyed.	18	—	25	—	18	—	7	—
b. Life is to be endured.	3	—	3	—	27	—	40	—
11. *a.* You should never question the word of your mother.[a]	1	9	1	4	15	22	23	25
b. Any mother can make mistakes, and you should question her word when it seems wrong.	19	104	27	85	31	104	27	61

O: original study.
R: replication.

NOTE. These are a few items from Form A of an instrument called "Views of Life" that is being developed for one of the phases of the project entitled "Style of Coping and Achievement—A Cross National Study of School Children" (by Robert F. Peck, A. Angelini, M. Cesa-Bianchi, Rogelio Díaz-Guerrero, R. J. Havighurst, U. Lehr, K. Miller, and N. Murakawa; mimeographed, 1965). These results portray the answers of freshman college students in the United States and third-year preparatory students in Mexico. The original study was done in Austin, Texas, and Toluca, Mexico; the replication was done in Austin and Mexico City.

[a] This question was modified between the first and second applications, and the result was to diminish the difference shown between the two cultures.

cans. Why? Perhaps if you are willing to endure life you may find it actually enjoyable; but, if you are out to enjoy it no matter what, you may find it terribly frustrating.

Let us now try to summarize in a few conclusions the main points that, with argument and some data, I have tried to make for you; and let me add to them some ideas that have not been specifically discussed but have been implied.

Americans have made gigantic discoveries regarding the theory and practice of economic development.

Mexicans and many other groups have discovered ways of life that may be contributions to the theory and practice of living.

Perhaps because of the self-sufficiency that economic success breeds, Americans may have become quite blind to the human and mental-health aspects necessarily involved and may even have dangerously neglected them.

Perhaps because of the well-being and inner happiness that an affiliative practice of living produces, Mexicans and other groups may have become quite blind to the contributions to the welfare of humans that have been made by the theory and practice of economic development and may have dangerously neglected them.

Proper research into these two different approaches to the problems of work and economic development, as well as intensive research on the sociocultural premises of each society and their effects upon their behavior, should prove very valuable in helping understand further some of the American's human and social problems and some of the Latin American's social and economic difficulties.

It would appear then that, when we can perceive in one sweep the intimate and gigantic puzzles of these sociocultural patternings and when their understanding can be easily imparted, we may be in the position to learn, as equals, from each others' experiences, something that we might want to do in regard to these human, social, and economic problems.

BIBLIOGRAPHY

Adorno, T. W., Else Frenkel-Brunswik, Daniel J. Levinson, and R. Nevitt Sanford, in collaboration with Betty Aron, Maria Hertz Levinson, and William Morrow. *The Authoritarian Personality*. New York: Harper and Brothers, 1950.

Ahumada Rodríguez, R., and E. Michelis. "Sindromes activo y pasivo a través de la Prueba de Frases Incompletas." In *La contribución de las ciencias psicológicas y del comportamiento al desarrollo social y económico de los pueblos*, edited by C. F. Hereford and L. Natalicio. Mexico City: Imprenta UNAM, 1967.

Alexander, Franz, and T. M. French. *Psychoanalytic Therapy*. New York: Ronald Press, 1946.

Allport, Gordon W. *Personality: A Psychological Interpretation*. New York: Henry Holt and Co., 1937.

Anderson, H. H., and G. L. Anderson. "A Cross-National Study of Teacher-Child Relations as Reported by Adolescent Children." Document presented at the Quinto Congreso Interamericano de Psicología, Mexico City, December, 1957.

———. "Cultural Reactions to Conflict, a Study of Adolescent Children in Four Countries: Germany, England, Mexico, United States." *The Journal of Social Psychology* 50 (1959): 47–55.

———. "Cultural Reactions to Conflict: A Study of Adolescent Children in Seven Countries." In *Psychological Approaches to Intergroup and International Understanding: A Symposium of the Third Interamerican Congress of Psychology*, edited by G. M. Gilbert, pp. 27–32. Austin, Texas: Interamerican Society of Psychology and Hogg Foundation for Mental Health, 1956.

———. "Symposium on Culture Components as a Significant Factor in Child Development: Image of the Teacher by Adolescent Children in Seven Countries." *American Journal of Orthopsychiatry* 31, no. 3 (1961): 481–492.

Bateson, Gregory. "Cultural Determinants of Personality." In *Personality and the Behavior Disorders*, edited by J. McV. Hunt, II, 714–735. New York: Ronald Press, 1944.

Benot, Eduardo. *Diccionario de ideas afines*. Buenos Aires: Ediciones Anaconda, 1942.

Bettelheim, Bruno, and M. B. Janowitz. *The Dynamics of Prejudice*. New York: Harper and Brothers, 1950.

Broom, Leonard. "Social Differentiation and Stratification." In *Sociology Today: Problems and Prospects*, edited by Robert K. Merton, Leonard Broom, and Leonard S. Cottrell, Jr., pp. 429–441. New York: Basic Books, 1960.

Brown, James A. *The Social Psychology of Industry: Human Relations in the Factory*. Harmondsworth, Eng., and Baltimore: Penguin, 1954.

Cantril, Malcolm. *Gauging Public Opinion*. Princeton: Princeton University Press, 1944.

Castaneda, Carlos. *The Teachings of Don Juan: A Yaqui Way of Knowledge*. Berkeley: University of California Press, 1968.

Coelho, G. V., and A. G. Steinbert, with the collaboration of E. D. Maldonado Sierra and R. Fernández Marina. "A Cross-Cultural Assessment of Coping Behavior: Student TAT Responses of Competent Adolescents in Maryland and Puerto Rico." Mimeographed, 1964.

Conrad, Herbert S. "The Validity of Personality Inventories in Military Practice." *Psychological Bulletin* 45, no. 5 (1948).

Delamater, John, Robert Hefner, Remi Clignet, and an International Editorial Committee chaired by Herbert Kelman and M. Brewster Smith, eds. *Social Psychological Research in Developing Countries. Journal of Social Issues* 24, no. 2 (1968).

Díaz-Guerrero, R. "The Active and the Passive Syndromes." *Revista Interamericana de Psicología* 1967, no. 1: 263–272.

———. "Diferencias sexuales en el desarrollo de la personalidad del escolar mexicano." Paper presented at the XIII Congreso Interamericano de Psicología, Panamá, December, 1971.

———. "Differences in Mexican and U.S. National Character and Their Implications for Public Health Practice." Paper presented at the Hidalgo Conference, Edinburg, Texas.

———. "Ensayos de psicología dinámica y científica." *Filosofía y Letras* 25, nos. 49–50 (1953): 97–150.

———. *Hacia una teoría histórico-bio-psico-socio-cultural del comportamiento humano*. Mexico City: Editorial F. Trillas, 1972.

———. "Interpreting Coping Styles across Nations from Sex and Social Class Differences." *International Journal of Psychology* 8, no. 3 (1973): 193–203.

————. "Mexican Assumptions about Interpersonal Relations." *ETC.: A Review of General Semantics* 16, no. 2 (Winter 1959): 185–188.

————. "Neurosis and the Mexican Family Structure." *American Journal of Psychiatry* 112, no. 6 (1955): 411–417.

————. "Occupational Values of Mexican School Children: A Comparative Intra and Cross Cultural Study." *Totus Homo* 4, no. 1 (1972): 18–26.

————. "Personality Development of Mexican School Children: A Research Proposal Submitted to the Foundations' Fund for Research in Psychiatry." *Anuario de Psicología* 3 (1964): 99–109.

————. "La semántica general de Korzybski." In *Memorias del Congreso Científico Mexicano*, XV, 531–535. Mexico City: UNAM, 1951.

————. "Socio-Cultural and Psychodynamic Processes in Adolescent Transition and Mental Health." In *Problems of Youth: Transition to Adulthood in a Changing World*, edited by Muzafer Sherif and Carolyn W. Sherif. Chicago: Aldine Publishing Co., 1965.

————. "Symposium on Culture and Child Development." *American Journal of Orthopsychiatry* 31, no. 3 (1961): 518–520.

————. "Una escala factorial de premisas histórico-socioculturales de la familia mexicana." *Interamerican Journal of Psychology* 6, nos. 3–4 (1972): 235–244.

Díaz-Guerrero, R., W. H. Holtzman, J. Swartz, L. Lara Tapia, and M. Tamm. "Simposio de estudios transculturales del desarrollo infantil en México y en los Estados Unidos en relación a factores de personalidad, cognición y clase social." In *Memorias del X Congreso Interamericano de Psicología*, edited by C. F. Hereford and L. Natalicio, pp. 121–164. Mexico City: Editorial F. Trillas, 1967.

Díaz-Guerrero, R., and Robert F. Peck. "Estilo de confrontación y aprovechamiento: Un programa de investigación." *Revista Interamericana de Psicología* 1967, no. 1: 127–136.

Dollard, John, Leonard Doob, Neal Miller, H. O. Mowrer, and R. Sears. *Frustration and Aggression.* New Haven: Yale University Press, 1943.

Eisenberg, P., and Paul Lazarsfeld. "The Psychological Effects of Unemployment." *Psychological Bulletin* 35 (1938): 358–390.

French, E. G. "Motivation as a Variable in Work-Partner Selection." *Journal of Abnormal and Social Psychology* 53 (1956): 96–99.

Fromm, Erich. *Man for Himself.* New York: Rinehart and Co., 1947.

————. *Psicoanálisis de la sociedad contemporánea.* Mexico City: Fondo de Cultura Económica, 1956.

Fromm, Erich, and Michael Maccoby. *Social Character in a Mexican Village.* Englewood Cliffs, New Jersey: Prentice-Hall, 1970.

Gallup, George H. *A Guide to Public Opinion Polls*. Princeton: Princeton University Press, 1944.

Goldstein, Kurt. *Human Nature*. Cambridge: Harvard University Press, 1940.

Gómez Robleda, José. *Imagen del mexicano*. Mexico City: Secretaría de Educación Pública, 1948.

Hayakawa, S. I. *Language in Action*. New York: Harcourt and Brace, 1943.

Hereford, C. F. "La dimensión actividad-pasividad en México y los Estados Unidos." Paper presented at the Primer Congreso Nacional de Psicología, Jalapa, Ver., Mexico, 1967. Mexico City: Imprenta Universitaria, UNAM, forthcoming.

Hereford, C. F., N. Selz, W. Stenning, and L. Natalicio. "A Cross-Cultural Comparison of the Active-Passive Dimension of Social Attitudes." *Interamerican Journal of Psychology* 1, no. 1 (March 1967): 33–39.

Holtzman, Wayne H., R. Díaz-Guerrero, J. Swartz, and L. Lara Tapia. "Cross-Cultural Longitudinal Research on Child Development: Studies of American and Mexican School Children." In *Minnesota Symposia on Child Psychology*, vol. 2. Minneapolis: University of Minnesota Press, 1968.

Horney, Karen. *New Ways in Psychoanalysis*. New York: W. W. Norton and Co., 1939.

Johnson, Wendell. *People in Quandaries*. New York and London: Harper and Brothers, 1946.

Kardiner, Abram. *The Individual and His Society*. New York: Columbia University Press, 1939.

Kelman, Herbert C. "Social-Psychological Research in Developing Countries." Mimeographed, 1965.

Keyes, Kenneth S. *How to Develop Your Thinking Ability*. New York: McGraw-Hill, 1950.

Kluckhohn, Clyde. "Values and Value Orientations in the Theory of Action: An Exploration in Definition and Classification." In *Toward a General Theory of Action*, edited by Talcott Parsons and Edward A. Shils, pp. 388–433. Cambridge: Harvard University Press, 1951.

Kluckhohn, F. R. "Dominant and Variant Value Orientations." In *Personality in Nature, Society and Culture*, edited by Clyde Kluckhohn, H. A. Murray, and D. F. Schneider, pp. 342–357. New York: Knopf, 1953.

Korzybski, Alfred. *Science and Sanity: An Introduction to Non-Aristotelian Systems and General Semantics*. Lakeville, Conn.: The Institute of General Semantics, 1948.

Kraines, S. H. *The Therapy of the Neuroses and Psychoses*. Philadelphia: Lea and Febiger, 1950.

Lagner, S. Thomas. "Psychophysiological Symptoms and Women's Status in Two Mexican Communities." Unpublished.

Lara Tapia, Luis, and María Luisa Morales. "Premisas socioculturales en tres comunidades indígenas de Tlaxcala." Mimeographed.

Lazarus, R. S. "A Program of Research in Psychological Stress." In *Festschrift for Gardner Murphy*, edited by J. G. Peatman and E. L. Hartley, pp. 313–329. New York: Harper and Brothers, 1960.

Lazarsfeld, Paul. "An Unemployed Village." *Character and Personality* 1 (1932): 147–151.

Lee, Irving J. *Language Habits in Human Affairs: An Introduction to General Semantics*. New York: Harper and Brothers, 1941.

Lewin, Kurt. *Dynamic Theory of Personality*. New York: McGraw-Hill, 1935.

Lewis, Oscar. *Five Families: Mexican Case Studies in the Culture of Poverty*. New York: Basic Books, 1959.

———. *La Vida: A Puerto Rican Family in the Culture of Poverty, San Juan and New York*. New York: Random House, 1966.

Liddell, H. S. "Conditioned Reflex Method and Experimental Neurosis." In *Personality and the Behavior Disorders*, edited by J. McV. Hunt. New York: Ronald Press, 1944.

López Velarde, Ramón. *Poesías completas*. 2d ed. Mexico City: Editorial Porrúa, 1957.

Luria, Alexander R. *Nature of Human Conflicts*. New York: Liveright, 1932.

McClelland, David C., and F. S. Apicella. "A Functional Classification of Verbal Reactions to Experimentally Induced Failure." *The Journal of Abnormal and Social Psychology* 40, no. 4 (1945).

McClelland, David C., J. W. Atkinson, R. A. Clark, and E. L. Lowell. *The Achievement Motive*. New York: Appleton Century Crofts, 1953.

McNemar, Quinn. "Opinion Attitude Methodology." *Psychological Bulletin* 43, no. 4 (1946).

Madsen, W. *Society and Health in the Lower Rio Grande Valley*. Austin, Texas: The Hogg Foundation for Mental Health, 1961.

Maldonado Sierra, E. D., Richard D. Trent, and R. Fernández Marina. "Neurosis and Traditional Family Beliefs in Puerto Rico." *International Journal of Social Psychiatry* 6 (1960): 237–246.

———. "Three Basic Themes in Mexican and Puerto Rican Family Values." *Journal of Social Psychology* 48 (1958): 167–181.

Maslow, Abraham H. *Motivation and Personality*. New York: Harper and Brothers, 1954.

Maslow, Abraham H., and R. Díaz-Guerrero, "Delinquency as a Value Disturbance." In *Festschrift for Gardner Murphy*, edited by J. G. Peatman and E. L. Hartley, pp. 228–229. New York: Harper and Brothers, 1960.

Maynes Puente, S. "Los mexicanos analizados por sí mismos." *Excélsior* (Mexico City), August 3, 1958.

Miller, Neal E. "Experimental Studies of Conflict." In *Personality and the Behavior Disorders*, edited by J. McV. Hunt. New York: Ronald Press, 1944.

Mowrer, O. H., and R. R. Lamoreaux. "Avoidance Conditioning and Signal Duration: A Study of Secondary Motivation and Reward." *Psychological Monographs* 54, no. 5 (1940).

Mowrer, O. H., and A. D. Ullman. "Time As a Determinant in Integrative Learning." *Psychology Review* 52, no. 2 (1945).

Murphy, Gardner. *Personality: A Biosocial Approach*. New York and London: Harper and Brothers, 1947.

Murphy, Lois B. *The Widening World of Childhood*. New York: Basic Books, 1962.

Pavlov, I. P. *Conditioned Reflexes*. New York: Oxford University Press, 1927.

Paz, Octavio. *El laberinto de la soledad*. Mexico City: Cuadernos Americanos, 1950.

Peck, Robert F. "A Comparison of the Value Systems of Mexican and American Youth." *Interamerican Journal of Psychology* 1 (1967): 41–50.

Peck, Robert F., A. L. Angelini, M. Cesa-Bianchi, R. Díaz-Guerrero, R. J. Havighurst, U. Lehr, K. Miller, and N. Murakawa. "Coping Style and Achievement: A Cross-National Study of School Children." Mimeographed, 1965.

Peck, Robert F., A. L. Angelini, R. Díaz-Guerrero, and C. F. Hereford. "Symposium on Problem-Solving Styles in Children: A Cross-National Study." In *Memorias del X Congreso Interamericano de Psicología*, edited by C. F. Hereford and L. Natalicio, pp. 223–268. Mexico City: Editorial F. Trillas, 1967.

Peck, Robert F., and R. Díaz-Guerrero. "The Meaning of Love in Mexico and the United States." *American Psychologist* 17 (1962): 329.

Possidente, William. "A Psychological Study of Public Opinion in Mexico." M.A. thesis, Mexico City College Library.

Ramos, Samuel. *El perfil del hombre y la cultura en México*. Mexico City: Pedro Robredo, 1938.

Rapoport, Anatol. "General Semantics: Its Place in Science." *ETC.: A Review of General Semantics* 16, no. 1 (1958): 80–97.

Reyes de Ahumada, I., and W. Stenning. "El rol desempeñado por la autoridad en los desacuerdos interpersonales: Un estudio comparativo en estudiantes mexicanos y norteamericanos." In *La contribución de las ciencias psicológicas y del comportamiento al desarrollo social y económico de los pueblos*, edited by C. F. Hereford and L. Natalicio. Mexico City: Imprenta UNAM, 1967.

Roethlisberger, Fritz J., and William J. Dickson. *Management and the Worker*. Cambridge: Harvard University Press, 1939.

Rogers, Carl R. *On Becoming a Person*. Boston: Houghton Mifflin, 1961.

————. *Psychotherapy and Personality Changes*. Chicago: University of Chicago Press, 1954.

Rojo I., Carmen. "El cambio de actitudes: Algunas consideraciones teóricas y un experimento psicosocial." Unpublished.

Romano, O. I. "Donship in a Mexican-American Community in Texas." *American Anthropologist* 62, no. 6 (1960): 966–976.

Rosenzweig, Saul. "An Outline of Frustration Theory." In *Personality and the Behavior Disorders*, edited by J. McV. Hunt. New York: Ronald Press, 1944.

Rubel, Arthur J. "Concepts of Disease in Mexican-American Culture." *American Anthropologist* 62, no. 5 (1960): 795–814.

Saul, Leon J. *Emotional Maturity*. Philadelphia: J. B. Lippincott and Co., 1947.

Secretaría de la Economía Nacional, Dirección General de Estadística. *Sexto censo de la población*. Mexico City, 1948.

Selye, Hans. *The Stress of Life*. New York: McGraw-Hill, 1956.

Stagner, Ross. *Psychology of Personality*. New York: McGraw-Hill, 1948.

Sullivan, Harry Stack. *Conceptions of Modern Psychiatry*. Washington, D.C.: The William Alanson White Psychiatric Foundation, 1947.

Tajfel, Henri. "Problems of International Cooperation in Social Psychological Research Concerned with New and Developing Countries." Mimeographed, 1964.

Wolfe, J. B. "Effectiveness of Token-Rewards for Chimpanzees." *Comparative Psychological Monographs* 12, no. 6 (1936).

Wolff, Werner. *Values and Personality*. New York: Grune and Stratton, 1951.

Zúñiga Oceguera, Victoria. "Estudios preliminares en México del inventario multifásico de la personalidad de Minnesota." M.A. thesis, Universidad Nacional Autónoma de México, 1958.

INDEX

Acculturation: in U.S.–Mexican border zone, 86, 87–88
Active endurer of stress (AES): motivations of, 124–125; and patterns of national character, 124; and sociocultural patterns, 122–123, 130–131
Active-passive dichotomy: and classification of sociocultures, 122; and resolution of stress, xviii, 121–122, 123, 131. *See also* Active endurer of stress; Passive endurer of stress
Adler, Alfred, 23; theory of, applied to Mexican circumstances, 37
AES. *See* Active endurer of stress
Aesthetic needs, 26, 30
Affiliation: importance of, in Mexican culture, 120
Affiliative needs: and human behavior, 25–27; and self-esteem, 40–42; and worker motivation, 36, 44–45. *See also* Love
Age and sex: and degree of respect, 105; and status, 101–102
Allport, Gordon W., 23
American Psychiatric Association, 14
Anderson, G. L., 90
Anderson, H. H., 90
Animism, 49–50, 51, 55, 60, 67–68, 72–74
Aristotle, 113
Artists: and self-actualization, 42–43; degree of respect for, 105
Attitude: and description of group behavior, 119
Authority figure: and formation of sociocultural premises, 116

Aztecs: social function of commerce among, 19

Beatnik: and the American socioculture, xix
Beggar: degree of respect for, 104
Behavior: multiple motivations for, 23–24
Behavioral science: and cultural analysis, xii–xiii
Behavioral threshold: and sociocultural premises, 117, 118
Belonging. *See* Affiliative needs
Bile: defined, 11
Biological integrity: preservation of, and human behavior, 25
Border zone: value pattern of, 87–88; view of respect in, 85–87
Boy. *See* Male child
Bragging: within friendship, 40–41; and self-esteem, 40; and sexual need, 33
Brown, James A.: on money and motivation, 35; on social function of factories, 44

Campbell, Donald, 21
Campo, Angel de, 41–42
Cantril, Malcolm, 114; on response to questionnaires, 53
Capitalism: and active-passive dichotomy, 123, 131
Castaneda, Carlos, xi
Catholicism: and active-passive dichotomy, 123, 131
Cervantes, Miguel de, 124

Child: behavior of, 102; destruction of self-esteem in, 38–39; and obedience, 10; personality development in, studied, 139–140; protection of, 25. *See also* Female child; Male child

Cognitive needs, 26, 30

Collateral family: degree of respect within, 102–103, 105

College students: suitability of, as research subjects, 79

Communication: social nature of, 116–117

Communitarian movement, 45

Congeniality: importance of, to interpersonal reality, 18–19

Conquest, the: influence of, on modern Mexico, xv–xvi; and Mexican inferiority complex, 37; in paintings, 42

Coping: research into, undertaken, 142; and study of stress, 131, 132, 141

"Coping Style and Achievement: A Cross-National Study of School Children": highlights of, 142–143

Core culture: value patterns of, 83–85, 87

Cosmos of respect: of American female, 99; of American male, 97; of Mexican female, 98; of Mexican male, 96; transcultural comparison of, for females, 106; transcultural comparison of, for males, 100

Courtship: and male-female roles, 8–9

Cross-cultural research: beginnings of, 138; elevance of, for developing nations, 144; takes root in Mexico, 139–141

Culture: approaches to analysis of, xi–xii; behavioral scientific analysis of, xii–xiii

Defense: research into, undertaken, 142; and study of stress, 131, 132

Delayed realization. *See* Reality principle

"Delinquency as a Value Disturbance," 15

Democracy: potential for, in Mexico, 110

Department of Statistics, 52

Development. *See* Socioeconomic development

Díaz-Guerrero, R., 91, 142; on behavior of children, 102; sociocultural investigations of, 89, 114

Dickson, William J., 35

Donism, 90

Don Quijote, 124

Economic position: and degree of respect, 103–104, 105

Economic values: and determination of respect, 109–110

Education: and female role, 7–8

Efficiency: importance of, in American culture, 120

Eisenberg, P., 121, 130; on fear of unemployment, 34

Entertainment: and worker motivation, 45–46

Equality: in American cultural pattern, xiv–xv, xvi, xvii; and respect, 109, 110

Europe: communitarian movement in, 45

External reality: and American psychoanalysis, 19–20; American and Mexican attitudes toward, 18

Factory: improvements in, and worker motivation, 43; social function of, 44–45

Family: fundamental propositions of, 3–4; and job insecurity, 34; sociocultural premises about, 137. *See also* Collateral family; Immediate family

Father. *See* Male

Female: activity-passivity of, in according respect, 107; concern of, for physical health, 33; cosmos of respect of, 98, 99, 108; cosmos of respect of, compared transculturally, 106; incidence of neurosis in, 10, 11; inhibition in, 55, 67; and love-power relationship, xvi; mental symptoms in, 54–55, 65–66; perception of sociocultural premises by, 13; and reality principle, 64; role expectations for, and neurosis, 11–12; role of, in family, 3–4; role of, as mother, 9, 10; role of, as wife, 9; satiation of affiliative needs by, as mother, 36; sociocultural premises about, 136; status of, 91–92; tolerance and objectivity in, 53–54, 62–63

Female child: pursuit of, in adolescence, 6; role expectations for, 5; socialization of, during adolescence, 7–9; undesirability of, 4

Fernández Marina, R., 14–16, 136

Festinger, Leon, 115

Festschrift for Gardner Murphy, 15

FFRP. *See* Foundations' Fund for Research in Psychiatry

Foundations' Fund for Research in Psychiatry (FFRP), 130; funds study of school children, 139

French, E. G., 120

French Revolution, ideals of, xiv

Freud, Sigmund, 23; theory of, and study of male neurosis, 11, 12

Friendship: and self-esteem, 40–42

Fromm, Erich, xi; on affiliative needs, 25–26; on social function of factories, 44–45

F-test, 81

Germany: as active endurer of stress, 124

Girl. *See* Female child

Girls' college, Monterrey: testing at, 80

Goldstein, Kurt, 30

Gómez Robleda, José, 13

Hereford, Carl F., xii

Hippie: and the American socioculture, xv, xix–xx

Hogg Foundation for Mental Health, 138

Holtzman, Wayne H., xii, 130, 141, 142; studies development in school children, 139

Horney, Karen, 23

Human needs: evaluation of, by profile, 31; hierarchy of, 24–31; multiplicity of, 23–24

Human values: and determination of respect, 109–110

Hunger: and worker motivation, 31–32

Hypochondria: among Mexicans, 32, 33

Ignorance. *See* Animism

Immediate family: degree of respect within, 102, 105

India: affective meaning of work in, 150

Indian, the: and the Conquest, xv

Industrial relations: and psychology, 21

Infant: and obedience, 9–10; veneration of, xvi–xvii, 9

Inferiority complex: in Mexican cultural pattern, 37–38

Inhibition: degree of, in Mexico City sample, 55, 66–67; explanation of, 71–72; and mental hygiene, 49; and plasticity-rigidity classification, 51, 59–60; and sociocultural forces, 56, 72

Integral development. *See* Self-actualization

Interpersonal reality: and congeniality, 18–19; effect of, on marital relations, 19; and togetherness, 20

Journal of Social Psychology, 15

Jung, Carl, 23

Kelman, Herbert C., 134, 134 n–135 n

Korzybskian identification, 49–50; explanation of, 72–74. *See also* Animism

Lagner, S. Thomas, 91–92

Lara Tapia, Luis, 135

Lazarsfeld, Paul, 121, 130; on fear of unemployment, 34

Lazarus, R. S., 122

Learned needs, 30–31

Learning theory: and sociocultural premises, 119

Lewin, Kurt, 71

Lewis, Oscar, xi

Life: American view of, xix–xx; Mexican view of, xx–xxi; view of, and active-passive dichotomy, 121; view of, and determination of respect,

111; view of, and work attitudes, 152, 155

Love: in American cultural pattern, xv; efficacy of, xviii; in Mexican cultural pattern, xvi–xvii; operational definition of, xvii; and power, xiii–xiv. *See also* Affiliative needs

McClelland, David C., xix, 120
Maccoby, Michael, xi
Machismo: and learned needs, 30–31
McNemar, Quinn, 53
Madsen, W., 90
Maldonado Sierra, E. D., 14–16, 136
Male: abuse of authority by, in family, 38; activity-passivity of, in according respect, 107; concern of, for physical health, 33; cosmos of respect of, 96, 97, 108; cosmos of respect of, compared transculturally, 100; incidence of neurosis in, 10, 11; inhibition in, 55, 67; and love-power relationship, xvi; and *machismo*, 30–31; mental symptoms in, 54–55, 65–66; perception of sociocultural premises by, 13; and reality principle, 64; role expectation for, and neurosis, 10–11, 12; role of, in family, 3, 4; role of, as father, 9; role of, as husband, 9; sociocultural premises about, 137; tolerance and objectivity in, 53–54, 62–63
Male child: desirability of, 4; protection of sister by, during adolescence, 8; role expectations for, 4–5; and sexuality, 5–7
Map-territory relationship: explained, 19 n
Marriage: interpersonal reality of, 19
Marxism-Leninism: and active-passive dichotomy, 123, 131
Maslow, Abraham H., 15; on behavior of children, 102; and hierarchy of human needs, 24–31
Maynes Puente, S., 41; on hunger and behavior, 31–32
Meaning atmosphere: and derivation of sociocultural premises, 113; phenomena associated with, 114
Menorvalía, 38 and n
Mental hygiene: and active-passive

dichotomy, 131–133; approach to study of, 48–49; and economic development, 155; factors of, 49–50; testing of, 50–52; and work attitudes, 152
Mental symptoms: degree of, in Mexico sample, 54–55, 65–66; explanation of, 71; factors contributing to, 55; and mental hygiene, 49; and plasticity-rigidity classification, 51, 59
Mexican-American: and love-power relationship, xxi. *See also* Border zone
Mexican Semantic Differential, 140
Minnesota Multiphasic Personality Inventory, 32
Money: and worker motivation, 35
Monterrey Technological Institute: testing at, 80
Mother. *See* female
Motivation: and hierarchy of human needs, 24–31; and human behavior, 23; multiple nature of, 23–24
Murphy, Lois B., 131, 141

National character: approach to study of, 78; patterns of, 121–124; and sociocultural premises, 109
National University of Mexico: interest in social psychology at, 142; testing at, 79–80
Neighbors: degree of respect for, 103, 105
Neurosis: and female role expectations, 11–12; incidence of, in Mexico City sample, 54; incidence of, and sex, 10, 11, 54–55; and male role expectations, 10–11, 12; and status, 91
Normal school, Mexico City: testing at, 80

Objectivity: degree of, in Mexico City sample, 53–54, 62–63; explanation of, 70; and mental hygiene, 49; and plasticity-rigidity classification, 51, 58
Occupation: and degree of respect, 103, 105
Oedipus complex, 11
Old people: veneration of, xvi, xvii

Osgood, Charles E., xii, 114, 115, 140; on attitude toward neurotics, 123

Paired comparison study, 143
Pan American College: testing at, 80
passive endurer of stress (PES): motivations of, 125; and patterns of national character, 124; and sociocultural patterns, 122–123, 130–131
Paz, Octavio, 45
Peace Corps, 148
Peck, Robert F., xii, 109, 131; designs stress research, 142; as pioneer in cross-cultural research, 138
"Personality Development in Mexican School Children": highlights of, 139–140
Personal safety: and worker motivation, 35–36
PES. See passive endurer of stress
Physical health: and worker motivation, 32–33
Physiological needs: and human behavior, 24; and worker motivation, 31–34
Plasticity: definition of, 49–50; and mental hygiene, 49
Population: distribution of, by occupation, 52, 61; and sampling techniques, 52
Power: in American cultural pattern, xv, xvi, xvii; efficacy of, xviii; and love, xiii–xiv; in Mexican cultural pattern, xvi–xvii; operational definition of, xvii
Preparatory schools, Mexican: testing at, 92
Preservation. See Biological integrity
Profile: defined, 31
Protestantism: and active-passive dichotomy, 123, 131
Psicoanálisis de la sociedad contemporánea, 44
Psychoanalysis: dynamic vs. status, 19–20; use of "reality" by, 17
Psychology: and industrial relations, 21
Puerto Rican Institute of Psychiatry, 14, 136
Puerto Rico: study of sociocultural premises of, 14–16

Puerto Rico, University of: testing at, 15

Questionnaire survey: composition of, in mental-hygiene study, 50–51; designing of, 135; and determination of sociocultural premises, 114, 115; form of, for cross-cultural study, 81; form of, for mental-hygiene study, 52, 74–77; form of, for respect-status study, 93; response to, in cross-cultural study, 83; response to, in mental-hygiene study, 52–53, 61; responses to, and sociocultural premises, 117; statistical analysis procedure, in cross-culture survey, 81–83; tabulation of results of, for respect-status study, 94–95; technique of, 50, 51–52; value of, as research technique, 88
Questionnaire threshold, 117, 118

Ramos, Samuel, 7; on Mexican inferiority complex, 37–38
Raza unida, la: and love-power relationship, xx, xxi
Reality: facing of, 17, 20; use of, in psychotherapy, 17. See also External reality; Interpersonal reality
Reality principle: degree of, in Mexico City sample, 54, 63–64; explanation of, 70–71; and mental hygiene, 49; and plasticity-rigidity classification, 51, 58–59
Reputation: and self-esteem, 29
Respect: and achievement, 110–111; associated meanings for, 80–81; as criterion of status, 91, 92; cross-cultural study of, 90; and human vs. economic values, 109–110; and occupation, 103, 105; and sociocultural presuppositions, 110; as topic for cross-cultural investigation, 78–79; view of, in border zone, 85–87; view of, in Mexican core culture, 84–85; view of, in Texas core culture, 83–84. See also Cosmos of respect
Rights of Man, 117
Rigidity: definition of, 49–50; and mental hygiene, 49

Roethlisberger, Fritz J., 35
Rogers, Carl R., 30
Romano, O. I., 90
Rubel, Arthur J., 90

Safety. See Personal safety
SCP. See Sociocultural premises
Self-actualization: and human behavior, 30; and worker motivation,
42–43
Self-esteem: and historical circum-
stances, 37; and human behavior,
27–29; influence of sociocultural
forces on, 38–39; and job insecurity,
34; and worker motivation, 36–42
Self-evaluation: and self-esteem, 27–
28
Selye, Hans, 123 n, 128 n
Semantic Differential, 140
Sex. See Age and sex
Sexuality: and male role expectations,
5–7
Sexual need: and worker motivation,
33
Social Character in a Mexican Village,
xi
Social psychology: relevance of, for developing nations, 144
Social Psychology of Industry, 44
Sociocultural premises (SCPs): and
authority figures, 116; definition of,
115–116; derivation of, 112–114;
determination of, 114, 115, 127–
128; facilitation of, 117–118; about
family, 137; and female role, 136;
hindrance of, 118–119; importance
of, 127; and learning theory, 119;
and male role, 137; and national
character, 109; perceptions of, by
sex, 13–14; permanency of, 119; for
Puerto Rico, studied, 14–16; social
functions of, 116–117; and socioeconomic development, 148–149;
about work, 153–154
Socioculture: classification of, by endurance of stress, 122; definition of,
115
Socioeconomic development: and emotionally adjusted society, 147; and
mental health, 155; and sociocultural premises, 148–149

Spanish language: embodiment of sub-
missive attitudes in, 10; translation
of "self-esteem" into, 28 and n
Stagner, Ross, 70
Status: criteria for, 92; and neurotic
symptoms, 91; as societal indicator,
91
Stress: American view of, 130; attitudes toward, and active-passive
dichotomy, xviii, 121–122; dealing
with, 128–129, 131–132, 141; definition of, 123 n, 128 n; and mental
health, 132–133; Mexican view of,
129–130
Stress of Life, The, 123 n, 128 n
Sullivan, Harry Stack, 20
Sweden: affective meaning of work in,
150
Syllogistic logic: and derivation of
sociocultural premises, 113–114

Tajfel, Henri, 139; research of, 134 and
n
T.A.T. pictures, 130
Teachings of Don Juan, xi
Technical skills: improvement of, and
worker motivation, 43–44
Texas: influence of Mexican heritage
upon, 79; view of respect in border
zone of, 85–87; view of respect in
core culture of, 83–84. See also
United States
Texas, University of: testing at, 80,
92
Third International, 117
"Three Basic Themes in Mexican and
Puerto Rican Family Values," 15
Tolerance: degree of, in Mexico City
sample, 53–54, 62–63; explanation
of, 69–70; and mental hygiene, 49;
and plasticity-rigidity classification,
51, 58
Transcultural research. See Cross-cultural research
Trent, Richard D.: study of sociocultural premises by, 14–16, 136; surveys sociocultural premises, 114

Unemployment: fear of, and worker
motivation, 33–34
United States: achievement orientation

of, and determination of respect, 110–111; active-autonomous orientation of, toward work, 149 n, 151–152; and active-passive dichotomy, xviii; affective meaning of work in, 149–150; age and sex and degree of respect in, 105; attitude toward stress in, 121, 130; economic position and degree of respect in, 103–104, 105; economic vs. human values in, 109–110; efficiency vs. affiliation in, 120; female cosmos of respect in, 99; job insecurity in, 34; male cosmos of respect in, 97; modern sociocultural trends in, xvii; occupation and degree of respect in, 103, 105; as "power-equality" socioculture, xiv–xv, xvi, xvii; respect for children in, 101–102; respect for family in, 102–103, 105; respect for friends in, 105; respect for neighbors in, 105; social activity in, and sex, 107; social function of factories in, 44; static view of psychoanalysis in, 19–20; view of life in, xix–xx. See also Texas

United States Department of Education: funds cross-cultural study of stress, 142

Values. See Economic values; Human values; Sociocultural premises

Veldman, Donald, 82

Virgin of Guadalupe: as psychological symbol, 12

Weighted representative sampling, 114; use of, in mental-hygiene survey, 52

Western Behavioral Sciences Institute, 140–141

Work: affective meaning of, in four cultures, 149–150; and affiliative ties, 151; and American success orientation, 151–152; attitudes toward, and active-passive dichotomy, 120, 143 n–144 n; attitudes toward, and mental health, 152; high productivity of Mexicans at, 146, 147–148; motivations for, 146–147; paired comparison study of, 143, 151; portrayal of, in Mexican popular wisdom, 21–22, 145, 146; satisfaction with, 22–23; and sociocultural premises, 148–149, 153–154

Written-test threshold, 117, 118

Zúñiga Oceguera, Victoria, 32